BREEZE

21

DESIGNS

By

KIM HARGREAVES

CREDITS

DESIGNS Kim Hargreaves

PHOTOGRAPHY Graham Watts

STYLING Kim Hargreaves

HAIR & MAKE-UP Diana Fisher

MODELS Hannah Wright & Kristie Stubley

EDITOR Kathleen Hargreaves

EDITORIAL DESIGN Graham Watts

LAYOUTS Angela Lin

PATTERNS Sue Whiting & Trisha McKenzie

ISBN–10 1-906487-04-1
ISBN–13 978-1-906487-04-1

CONTENTS

THE
DESIGNS

LOVE-WORN PRINTS, FADED BLOOMS AND CANDY HUES
EVOKE MEMORIES OF CHERISHED SUMMER DAYS

WISPY — AN A-LINE JACKET WITH OVERSIZED BUTTONS

RUBY — BELTED JACKET WITH GENEROUS BACK NECK

WILLOW — A TUNIC WITH DEEP SCOOPED NECKLINE

ASH — STRIPED SLOUCHY HAT

GEORGIE — HOODED CARDIGAN

PEACHES — SLOUCHY CROCHET BERET

DOLLY — CARDIGAN WITH FLOUNCED MOSS STITCH HEM & CONTRAST DETAIL

BLITHE — CAPPED SLEEVE BUTTON THROUGH VEST

STEVIE — BOXY CARDIGAN WITH SINGLE BUTTON

HUSH — SEMI FITTED CARDIGAN WORKED IN DOUBLE MOSS STITCH

KIT — CARDIGAN WITH OVERSIZED BUTTONS

ROSE — SWEATER WITH GENEROUS BACK NECK

BUTTERCUP — PRETTY SHRUG WITH BUTTON DETAIL

Perfect

FRANKIE — BOYFRIEND CARDIGAN WITH POCKET DETAILS

ALI – NEAT JACKET WORKED IN A BASKET WEAVE STITCH

DAISY — A PREPPY CARDIGAN WITH SHORT SLEEVES & CONTRAST TRIM

LAVENDER — A CARDIGAN WITH LACE EDGING

STEVIE — BOXY CARDIGAN WORKED IN GARTER STITCH

PEACHES — SLOUCHY CROCHET BERET

GEORGIE — RELAXED CARDIGAN WITH HOOD

DEVON — STRIPED SLOUCHY SWEATER WITH WIDE NECKLINE

BAY — JACKET WITH FLOUNCE EDGING & GARTER STITCH TRIM

LILAC — OPENWORK CARDIGAN WITH LACY PEPLUM

ASH — STRIPED SLOUCHY HAT

PURE — SWEATER WITH FLOUNCED HEMLINE

THE PATTERNS

LAVENDER
CARDIGAN WITH LACE EDGINGS & DOUBLE BUTTONS

Recommendation
Suitable for the knitter with a little experience.
Please see pages 36 & 37 for photographs.

	XS	S	M	L	XL	XXL	
To fit	**81**	**86**	**91**	**97**	**102**	**107**	cm
bust	32	34	36	38	40	42	in

Rowan Handknit Cotton

11	12	12	13	14	15	x 50gm

Photographed in Antique

Buttons – 2

Needles
1 pair 3¾ mm (no 9) (US 5) needles
1 pair 4 mm (no 8) (US 6) needles
Cable needle

Tension
21 sts and 28 rows to 10 cm measured over
pattern using 4 mm (US 6) needles.

Special abbreviation
MP = Make picot: cast on 1 st, cast off 1 st.
(See information page for details)

Lower edging (worked in one piece)
Cast on 21 (21: 22: 22: 23: 23) sts using
3¾ mm (US 5) needles.
Knit 1 row.
Foundation row: K5, K2tog, K2, yo, K1,
K2tog, yo, K2tog, K1, yo, K6 (6: 7: 7: 8: 8).
Row 1 (RS): Sl 1, K5 (5: 6: 6: 7: 7), yo,
slip the yo of the previous row, K2, inc
(by knitting into front and back of yo of
previous row), K3, sl next 2 sts onto cn
and hold in front, K3, then K2 from cn,
yo, K2tog, K1.
Row 2: Cast on 2 sts and cast off 2 sts, K
until there are 7 sts on right needle, K2tog,
yo, K2tog, K4, (K1, P1) into both yo loops
together, as if they were a single loop, K6 (6: 7:
7: 8: 8).
Row 3: Sl 1, K4 (4: 5: 5: 6: 6), K2tog, yo,
K2tog, K10, yo, K2tog, K1.
Row 4: K5, (yo, K1) twice, K2tog, yo, K2tog,
K3, yo, drop the yo of previous row off needle,
K6 (6: 7: 7: 8: 8).
Row 5: Sl 1, K5 (5: 6: 6: 7: 7), (K1, P1) into
the yo of previous row, K7, inc, K1, inc, K2,
yo, K2tog, K1.
Row 6: Cast on 2 sts and cast off 2 sts, K
until here are 5 sts on right needle, yo, K2, yo,
K2tog, K1, yo, (K1, K2tog, yo, K2tog) twice,
K5 (5: 6: 6: 7: 7).
Row 7: Sl 1, K5 (5: 6: 6: 7: 7), yo, drop the
yo of previous row off needle, K6, (yo, K2tog,
K1) 4 times.
Row 8: K5, (yo, K2tog, K1) 3 times, yo,
K2tog, K2, (K1, P1) into the yo of previous
row, K6 (6: 7: 7: 8: 8).
Row 9: Sl 1, K4 (4: 5: 5: 6: 6), K2tog, yo,
K2tog, K5, (yo, K2tog, K1) 4 times.
Row 10: Cast on 2 sts and cast off 2 sts, K
until there are 5 sts on right needle, (yo, K2tog,
K1) 3 times, yo, K2tog, K2, yo, drop the yo of
previous row off needle, K6 (6: 7: 7: 8: 8).
Row 11: Sl 1, K5 (5: 6: 6: 7: 7), (K1, P1) into the
yo of previous row, K6, (yo, K2tog, K1) 4 times.
Row 12: K5, (yo, K2tog, K1) 4 times, K2tog,
yo, K2tog, K5 (5: 6: 6: 7: 7).
Row 13: Work as row 7.

Row 14: Cast on 2 sts and cast off 2 sts,
K until there are 5 sts on right needle, (yo,
K2tog, K1) 3 times, yo, K2tog, K2, (K1, P1)
into the yo of previous row, K6 (6: 7: 7: 8: 8).
Row 15: Work as row 9.
Row 16: K5, (yo, K2tog, K1) 3 times, yo,
K2tog, K2, yo, drop the yo of previous row off
needle, K6 (6: 7: 7: 8: 8).
Row 17: Sl 1, K5 (5: 6: 6: 7: 7), (K1, P1) into
the yo of previous row, K6, yo, (K2tog, K1)
twice, (yo, K2tog, K1) twice.
Row 18: Cast on 2 sts and cast off 2 sts,
K until here are 5 sts on right needle, yo,
K2tog, K1, K2tog, yo, K2tog, K1, yo, K3,
K2tog, yo, K2tog, K5 (5: 6: 6: 7: 7).
Row 19: Sl 1, K5 (5: 6: 6: 7: 7), yo, drop the
yo of previous row off needle, K7, yo, K2tog,
K2, (yo, K2tog, K1) twice.
Row 20: K5, yo, (K2tog) twice, yo, K2tog, K1,
yo, K5, (K1, P1) into the yo of previous row,
K6 (6: 7: 7: 8: 8).
Row 21: Sl 1, K4 (4: 5: 5: 6: 6), K2tog, yo,
K2tog, K7, (K2tog, K1) twice, yo, K2tog, K1.
Row 22: K5, K2tog, K2, yo, K1, K2tog, yo,
K2tog, K1, yo, drop the yo of previous row
off needle, K6 (6: 7: 7: 8: 8).
Repeat rows 1 – 22.
Work 10 (11: 12: 13: 14: 15) repeats of
the edging and then work fi rst row again.
Note: each patt repeat measures approx
8 cm, so edging should measure approx
80 (88: 96: 104: 112: 120) cm.
Cast off.
Place a marker 59 (66: 73: 80: 87: 94) rows
in from each end of the edging, i.e. 59 (66: 73:
80: 87: 94) rows for each front and 102 (110:
118: 126: 134: 142) rows for back.

BACK
With RS of edging facing, using 4 mm
(US 6) needles, pick up and knit 76 (80:
86: 90: 96: 104) sts evenly across the top
(straight) edge of edging between fi rst
and second markers and P 1 row, ending
with a WS row..
Row 1 (RS): Knit.

Row 2: P1 (3: 6: 2: 5: 3), *yrn, P2, then lift the yarn over the last 2 sts and off right needle, P4, rep from * to last 3 (5: 8: 4: 7: 5) sts, yrn, P2, then lift the yarn over the last 2 sts and off right needle, P1 (3: 6: 2: 5: 3).
Row 3: Knit.
Row 4: Purl.
Row 5: Knit.
Row 6: P4 (6: 3: 5: 2: 6), *yrn, P2, then lift the yarn over the last 2 sts and off right needle, P4, rep from * to last 6 (8: 5: 7: 4: 8) sts, yrn, P2, then lift the yarn over the last 2 sts and off right needle, P4 (6: 3: 5: 2: 6).
Row 7: Knit
Row 8: Purl.
These 8 rows form the patt and are repeated throughout.
Keeping patt correct throughout, inc 1 st at each end of next row and 4 foll 10th rows, taking extra sts into patt, and ending with a **RS** row.
86 (90: 96: 100: 106: 114) sts .
Cont straight until back measures 21 (21: 22: 22: 22: 23) cm from pick-up row, ending with a WS row.

Shape armholes
Cast off 4 sts at beg of next 2 rows.
78 (82: 88: 92: 98: 106) sts.
Dec 1 st at each end of next 5 (5: 5: 5: 7: 7) rows, then on 1 (1: 2: 2: 1: 3) foll alt rows, and then on 1 foll 4th row.
64 (68: 72: 76: 80: 84) sts.
Work straight until armhole measures 16.5 (17.5: 17.5: 18.5: 19.5: 20.5) cm, ending with a WS row.

Shape back neck and shoulders
Work 17 (18: 20: 21: 23: 24) sts and turn, leaving rem sts on a holder.
Work each side of neck separately.
Dec 1 st at neck edge on next 3 rows, ending with a WS row. 14 (15: 17: 18: 20: 21) sts.
Cast off 4 (5: 5: 6: 6: 7) sts at beg and dec 1 st at end of next row.
Work 1 row.
Cast off 4 (4: 5: 5: 6: 6) sts at beg and dec 1 st at end of next row.
Work 1 row.
Cast off rem 4 (4: 5: 5: 6: 6) sts.
With RS facing rejoin yarn to rem sts, cast off centre 30 (32: 32: 34: 34: 36) sts, patt to end.
Complete to match fi rst side, reversing shapings.

LEFT FRONT
With RS of edging facing, using 4 mm (US 6) needles, pick up and knit 49 (51: 54: 57: 60: 64) sts evenly across the top (straight) edge of edging between second marker and centre front edge.
Next row (WS): MP, K until 20 (20: 20: 21: 21: 21) sts on right needle, P to end.
Row 1 (RS): Knit.
Row 2: K20 (20: 20: 21: 21: 21), P2, * yrn, P2, then lift the yarn over the last 2 sts and off right needle, P4, rep from * to last 3 (5: 8: 4: 7: 5) sts, yrn, P2, then lift the yarn over the last 2 sts and off right needle, P1 (3: 6: 2: 5: 3).
Row 3: Knit.
Row 4: MP, K until 20 (20: 20: 21: 21: 21) sts on right needle, P to end.
These rows set the stitches for the pattern (as given for back) and the garter stitch edging with a picot worked every 4th row.
Keeping pattern and edging correct throughout cont as folls:
Work 2 rows.
Shape front neck and side edge as folls:
Next row(RS)(dec): Patt to last 22 (22: 22: 23: 23: 23) stitches, K2tog tbl, K to end. 48 (50: 53: 56: 59: 63) sts.
Work 1 row.
Cont shaping front edge by dec 1 st as before on every foll 8th row (from last dec) and **at the same time** shape side edge by inc 1 st at beg of next row and 4 foll 10th rows.
48 (50: 53: 56: 59: 63) sts.
Keeping neck shaping correct cont in patt until front matches back to armhold shaping, ending with a WS row.
Shape armhole
Keeping neck shaping correct, cast off 4 sts at beg of next row.
Work 1 row.
Dec 1 st at armhole edge on next 5 (5: 5: 5: 7: 7) rows, then on 1 (1: 2: 2: 1: 3) foll alt rows, and then on 1 foll 4th row.
Cont shaping front until 32 (34: 37: 40: 41: 42) sts rem.
Cont until front matches back to beg of shoulder shaping, ending with a WS row.
Shape shoulder
Cast off 4 (5: 5: 6: 6: 7) sts at beg of next row and 4 (5: 5: 6: 6: 6) sts at beg of foll alt row.
Work 1 row.

Cast off 4 (4: 5: 5: 6: 6), inc in next stitch, work to end, ending with a **RS** row.
21 (21: 21: 22: 22: 22) sts.
Keeping picot correct work a further 38 (40: 40: 42: 42: 44) rows ending at outside edge.
Shape centre back edge
Work to last 4 sts, wrap next stitch, turn and K to end.
Work to last 9 sts, wrap next stitch, turn and K to end.
Work to last 14 sts, wrap next stitch, turn and K to end.
Cast off.

RIGHT FRONT
With RS of edging facing, using 4 mm (US 6) needles, pick up and knit 49 (51: 54: 57: 60: 64) sts evenly across the top (straight) edge of edging from centre front edge to first marker.
Next row (WS) (buttonhole): P to last 20 (20: 20: 21: 21: 21) sts, K4, cast off next 3, K4 (5 sts now on needle after cast off sts), cast off next 3 sts, K to end.
Row 1 (RS): MP, K to end, casting on 3 sts over those cast off on previous row.
Row 2: P1 (3: 6: 2: 5: 3), *yrn, P2, then lift the yarn over the last 2 sts and off right needle, P4, rep from * to last 24 (24 :24: 25: 25: 25) sts, yrn, P2, then lift the yarn over the last 2 sts and off right needle, P2, K to end.
Row 3: Knit.
Row 4: P to last 20 (20: 20: 21: 21: 21) sts, K to end.
These rows set the stitches for the pattern (as given for back) and the garter stitch edging with a picot worked every 4th row.
Keeping pattern and edging correct throughout cont as folls:
Work 2 rows.
Shape front neck and side edge as folls:
Next row(RS)(dec): K 20 (20: 20: 21: 21: 21), K2tog, patt to end. 48 (50: 53: 56: 59: 63) sts.
Complete to match fi rst side reversing shapings.

SLEEVES (both alike)
Lower edging
Cast on 11 (11: 12: 12: 13: 13) stitches using 3 ¾ mm (US 5) needles.
Row 1 (RS): MP, K to end.
Row 2: Knit.

Rep these 2 rows until 88 (92: 96: 100: 104: 108) rows in all completed, ending with a WS row.

Cast off but do not break yarn.

With RS of edging facing, using 4 mm (US 6) needles, pick up and knit 52 (54: 56: 58: 60: 62) sts evenly across the top (straight) edge of edging and P 1 row, ending with a WS row.

Row 1 (RS): Knit.

Row 2: P1 (2: 3: 4: 5: 6), *yrn, P2, then lift the yarn over the last 2 sts and off right needle, P4, rep from * to last 3 (4: 5: 6: 7: 8) sts, yrn, P2, then lift the yarn over the last 2 sts and off right needle, P1 (2: 3: 4: 5: 6).

Row 3: Knit.

Row 4: Purl.

Row 5: Knit.

Row 6: P4 (5: 6: 1: 2: 3), *yrn, P2, then lift the yarn over the last 2 sts and off right needle, P4, rep from * to last 6 (7: 8: 3: 4: 5) sts, yrn, P2, then lift the yarn over the last 2 sts and off right needle, P4 (5: 6: 1: 2: 3).

Row 7: Knit

Row 8: Purl.

These 8 rows form the patt and are repeated throughout.

Keeping patt correct, inc 1 st at each end of next row and every foll 10th row to 64 (62: 64: 64: 66: 66) sts and then for the 5 larger sizes every foll 12th row to – (66: 68: 70: 72: 74) sts.

64 (66: 68: 70: 72: 74) sts.

Cont until sleeve measures 27 (28: 29: 30: 31: 32) cm from top of edging, ending with a WS row.

Shape sleeve top

Cast off 4 sts at beg of next 2 rows.

56 (58: 60: 62: 64: 66) sts.

Dec 1 st at each end of next 3 rows, then on 3 foll alt rows and then on 4 (4: 4: 5: 5: 5) foll 4th rows, ending with a **RS** row.

36 (38: 40: 40: 42: 44) sts.

Work 1 row.

Dec 1 st at each end of next row and 1 (2: 2: 2: 2: 2) foll alt rows and then on every row until 22 (22: 24: 24: 26: 28) sts rem.

Cast off.

MAKING UP

Press all pieces using a warm iron over a damp cloth.

Join both shoulder seams using back stitch.

Join the cast off ends of the extended front bands together and slip stitch into place around the back neck.

Join side and sleeve seams.

Set sleeves into armholes.

Sew on buttons.

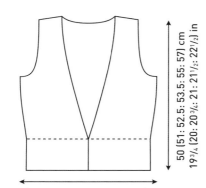

50 (51: 52.5: 53.5: 55: 57) cm
19³/₄ (20: 20³/₄: 21: 21¹/₂: 22¹/₂) in

41 (43: 45.5: 47.5: 50.5: 54.5) cm
16¹/₄ (17: 18: 18³/₄: 20: 21¹/₂) in

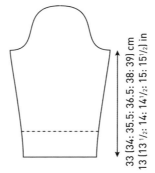

33 (34: 35.5: 36.5: 38: 39) cm
13 (13¹/₂: 14: 14¹/₂: 15: 15¹/₂) in

KIT

TEXTURED JACKET WITH DEEP RAGLANS & OVERSIZED BUTTONS

Recommendation

Suitable for the knitter with a little experience.
Please see pages 6, 10 & 26 for photographs.

	XS	S	M	L	XL	XXL	
To fit	**81**	**86**	**91**	**97**	**102**	**109**	**cm**
bust	32	34	36	38	40	43	in

Rowan All Seasons Cotton

14   14   15   16   17   18   x 50gm

Photographed in Bark

Buttons – 3

Needles

1 pair 4mm (no 8) (US 6) needles
1 pair 5mm (no 6) (US 8) needles

Tension

19 sts and 25 rows to 10 cm measured over
pattern using 5mm (US 8) needles.

BACK

Cast on 101 (105: 111: 115: 121: 129) sts
using 5mm (US 8) needles.
Row 1 (RS): P0 (0: 1: 1: 0: 0), *K1 tbl, P1; rep
from * to last 1 (1: 0: 0: 1: 1) st, (K1 tbl) 1 (1:
0: 0: 1: 1) times.
Row 2: Knit.
These 2 rows form patt.
Work in patt for 72 (72: 72: 74: 74: 74) rows
more, ending with a WS row. (Back should
measure 30 (30: 30: 31: 31: 31) cm.)
Shape raglan armholes
Keeping patt correct, cast off 8 (8: 8: 9: 9:
10) sts at beg of next 2 rows.
85 (89: 95: 97: 103: 109) sts.
Next row (RS): P2 (2: 1: 2: 1: 1), (P2tog) 0 (0:
1: 0: 1: 1) times, patt to last 2 (2: 3: 2: 3: 3)
sts, (P2tog tbl) 0 (0: 1: 0: 1: 1) times, P2 (2:
1: 2: 1: 1).
Next row: Knit.
Next row: P1, P2tog, patt to last 2 sts, P2tog
tbl, P1.
83 (87: 91: 95: 99: 105) sts.
Next row: Knit.
Rep last 2 rows 30 (31: 32: 33: 34: 36) times
more, ending with a WS row.
Cast off rem 23 (25: 27: 29: 31: 33) sts.

POCKET LININGS (make 2)

Cast on 23 (23: 25: 25: 27: 27) sts using
5mm (US 8) needles.
Beg with a P row, work in rev st st for 26 rows,
ending with a WS row.
Leave sts on a holder.

Pattern note: When knitting fronts, it is
advisable to join in new balls of yarn at side
seam or armhole edge so that front opening
edge remains neat and tidy as there are no
front opening edgings added afterwards.

LEFT FRONT

Cast on 58 (60: 63: 65: 68: 72) sts using
5mm (US 8) needles.
Row 1 (RS): P0 (0: 1: 1: 0: 0), *K1 tbl, P1;
rep from * to last 12 sts, P12.

Row 2: Knit.
Row 3: P0 (0: 1: 1: 0: 0), *K1 tbl, P1; rep
from * to last 12 sts, K12.
Row 4: P12, K to end.
These 4 rows set the sts – front opening edge
12 sts in ridge patt with all other sts in patt
as given for back.
Work in patt for 28 rows more, ending with
a WS row.
Place pocket
Next row (RS): Patt 8 (9: 10: 11: 12: 13) sts,
slip next 23 (23: 25: 25: 27: 27) sts onto a
holder and, in their place, patt across 23 (23:
25: 25: 27: 27) sts of first pocket lining, patt
to end.
Cont straight until left front matches back to beg
of raglan armhole shaping, ending with a WS row.
Shape raglan armhole
Keeping patt correct, cast off 8 (8: 8: 9: 9:
10) sts at beg of next row.
50 (52: 55: 56: 59: 62) sts.
Work 1 row.
Working all raglan armhole decreases as
set by back, dec 1 st at raglan armhole
edge of 3rd (3rd: next: 3rd: next: next)
and foll 23 (24: 26: 25: 27: 29) alt rows.
26 (27: 28: 30: 31: 32) sts.
Work 1 row, ending with a WS row.
Shape neck
Next row (RS): P1, P2tog, patt 9 (9: 9: 11:
11: 11) sts and turn, leaving rem 14 (15: 16:
16: 17: 18) sts on a holder.
11 (11: 11: 13: 13: 13) sts.
Keeping patt correct, dec 1 st at neck
edge of next 4 rows, then on foll 1 (1: 1: 2:
2: 2) alt rows **and at same time** dec 1 st at
raglan armhole edge of 2nd and every foll
alt row.
3 sts.
Work 1 row.
Next row (RS): P3tog.
Next row: K1 and fasten off.

RIGHT FRONT

Cast on 58 (60: 63: 65: 68: 72) sts using
5mm (US 8) needles.

Row 1 (RS): P12, *P1, K1 tbl; rep from * to last 0 (0: 1: 1: 0: 0) st, P0 (0: 1: 1: 0: 0).
Row 2: Knit.
Row 3: K12, *P1, K1 tbl; rep from * to last 0 (0: 1: 1: 0: 0) st, P0 (0: 1: 1: 0: 0).
Row 4: K to last 12 sts, P12.
These 4 rows set the sts – front opening edge 12 sts in ridge patt with all other sts in patt as given for back.
Work in patt for 28 rows more, ending with a WS row.

Place pocket
Next row (RS): Patt 27 (28: 28: 29: 29: 32) sts, slip next 23 (23: 25: 25: 27: 27) sts onto a holder and, in their place, patt across 23 (23: 25: 25: 27: 27) sts of second pocket lining, patt to end.
Cont straight until right front matches back to beg of raglan armhole shaping, ending with a **WS** row.

XS, S and M sizes only
Next row (buttonhole row) (RS): K4, cast off 3 sts (to make a buttonhole – cast on 3 sts over these cast-off sts on next row), patt to end.
Making a further 2 buttonholes in this way on 24th and foll 24th row and noting that no further reference will be made to buttonholes, cont as folls:

All sizes
Work 0 (0: 0: 1: 1: 1) row, ending with a RS row.

Shape raglan armhole
Keeping patt correct, cast off 8 (8: 8: 9: 9: 10) sts at beg of next row.
50 (52: 55: 56: 59: 62) sts.

L, XL and XXL sizes only
Next row (buttonhole row) (RS): K4, cast off 3 sts (to make a buttonhole – cast on 3 sts over these cast-off sts on next row), patt to last · (·: ·: 2: 3: 3) sts, (P2tog tbl) · (·: ·: 0: 1: 1) times, P· (·: ·: 2: 1: 1).
Making a further 2 buttonholes in this way on · (·: ·: 24th: 24th: 28th) and foll · (·: ·: 24th: 24th: 28th) row and noting that no further reference will be made to buttonholes, cont as folls:
Work 1 row, ending with a WS row.

All sizes
Working all raglan armhole decreases as set by back, dec 1 st at raglan armhole edge of 3rd (3rd: next: next: next: next) and foll 23 (24: 26: 25: 26: 28) alt rows.
26 (27: 28: 30: 31: 32) sts.
Work 1 row, ending with a WS row.

Shape neck
Next row (RS): Patt 14 (15: 16: 16: 17: 18) sts and slip these sts onto a holder, patt to last 3 sts, P2tog tbl, P1.
11 (11: 11: 13: 13: 13) sts.
Keeping patt correct, dec 1 st at neck edge of next 4 rows, then on foll 1 (1: 1: 2: 2: 2) alt rows and at same time dec 1 st at raglan armhole edge of 2nd and every foll alt row. 3 sts.
Work 1 row.
Next row (RS): P3tog.
Next row: K1 and fasten off.

SLEEVES (both alike)
Cast on 55 (57: 59: 59: 61: 65) sts using 5mm (US 8) needles.
Row 1 (RS): P1, *K1 tbl, P1; rep from * to end.
Row 2: Knit.
These 2 rows form patt.
Cont in patt for 4 rows more, ending with a WS row.
Inc 1 st at each end of next and foll 6th row, then on 6 (7: 8: 8: 9: 11) foll 4th rows, then on foll 12 (11: 10: 11: 10: 8) alt rows, taking inc sts into patt. 95 (97: 99: 101: 103: 107) sts.
Work 3 rows, ending with a WS row.
(Sleeve should measure 25.5 (26: 27: 28: 29: 30) cm.)

Shape raglan
Keeping patt correct, cast off 8 (8: 8: 9: 9: 10) sts at beg of next 2 rows.
79 (81: 83: 83: 85: 87) sts.
Working all raglan decreases in same way as given for back raglan armhole decreases, dec 1 st at each end of next (next: next: 3rd: 3rd: 3rd) and 0 (0: 0: 1: 1: 3) foll 4th rows, then on foll 29 (30: 31: 29: 30: 28) alt rows.
19 (19: 19: 21: 21: 23) sts.
Work 1 row, ending with a WS row.

Left sleeve only
Dec 1 st at each end of next row, then cast off 5 (5: 5: 6: 6: 6) sts at beg of foll row.
12 (12: 12: 13: 13: 15) sts.
Dec 1 st at beg of next row, then cast off 6 (6: 6: 6: 6: 7) sts at beg of foll row, ending with a WS row.

Right sleeve only
Cast off 6 (6: 6: 7: 7: 7) sts at beg and dec 1 st at end of next row.
12 (12: 12: 13: 13: 15) sts.
Work 1 row.
Cast off 6 (6: 6: 6: 6: 7) sts at beg and dec 1 st at end of next row.
Work 1 row, ending with a WS row.

Both sleeves
Cast off rem 5 (5: 5: 6: 6: 7) sts.

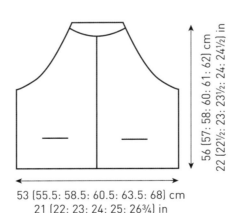

53 (55.5: 58.5: 60.5: 63.5: 68) cm
21 (22: 23: 24: 25: 26¾) in

56 (57: 58: 60: 61: 62) cm
22 (22½: 23: 23½: 24: 24½) in

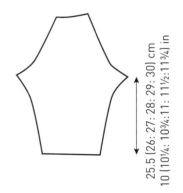

25.5 (26: 27: 28: 29: 30) cm
10 (10¼: 10¾:11: 11½: 11¾) in

MAKING UP

Pin out pieces and press carefully following instructions on ball band.

Join all raglan seams using back stitch, or mattress stitch if preferred.

Collar

With RS facing and using 4mm (US 6) needles, slip 14 (15: 16: 16: 17: 18) sts from right front holder onto right needle, rejoin yarn and pick up and knit 10 (10: 10: 12: 12: 12) sts up right side of neck, 17 (17: 17: 19: 19: 21) sts from top of right sleeve, 23 (25: 27: 29: 31: 33) sts from back, 17 (17: 17: 19: 19: 21) sts from top of left sleeve, and 10 (10: 10: 12: 12: 12) sts down left side of neck, then patt 14 (15: 16: 16: 17: 18) sts left on left front holder.

105 (109: 113: 123: 127: 135) sts.

Row 1 (WS of body): Patt 12 sts, K1, *P1, K1; rep from * to last 12 sts, patt 12 sts.

Row 2: Patt 12 sts, P1, *K1, P1; rep from * to last 12 sts, patt 12 sts.

These 2 rows set the sts – front opening edge 12 sts still in ridge st with all other sts now in rib.

Cont as set for 8 rows more.

Change to 5mm (US 8) needles.

Cont as set until collar measures 18 cm from pick-up row, ending with RS of body facing for next row.

Cast off in patt.

Pocket tops (both alike)

Slip 23 (23: 25: 25: 27: 27) sts from pocket holder onto 4mm (US 6) needles and rejoin yarn with RS facing.

Beg with a P row, work in rev st st for 3 rows, ending with a **RS** row.

Cast off knitwise (on **WS**).

Sew pocket linings in place on inside, then neatly sew down ends of pocket tops.

Join side and sleeve seams.

Sew on buttons.

WISPY

DOUBLE MOSS STITCH A-LINE JACKET WITH OVERSIZED BUTTONS

Recommendation

Suitable for the novice knitter.
Please see pages 8 & 9 for photographs.

	XS	S	M	L	XL	XXL	
To fit	**81**	**86**	**91**	**97**	**102**	**109**	**cm**
bust	32	34	36	38	40	43	in

Rowan Summer Tweed

8 9 9 10 11 11 x 50gm
Photographed in Navy

Buttons – 2 large

Needles

1 pair 4 mm (no 8) (US 6) needles
1 pair 4 ½ mm (no 7) (US 7) needles

Tension

18 sts and 25 rows to 10 cm measured over double moss stitch using 4 ½ mm (US 7) needles.

Pattern note: When knitting fronts, it is advisable to join in new balls of yarn at side seam or armhole edge so that front opening edge remains neat and tidy as there are no front opening edgings added afterwards.

BACK

Cast on 87 (91: 95: 99: 105: 113) sts using 4 ½ mm (US 7) needles and work in **double moss st** setting the sts as folls:
Row 1 (RS): P1 (1: 1: 1: 0: 0), (K1, P1) to last 0 (0: 0: 0: 1: 1) sts, K0 (0: 0: 0: 1: 1).
Row 2: K1 (1: 1: 1: 0: 0), (P1, K1) to last 0 (0: 0: 0: 1: 1) sts, P0 (0: 0: 0: 1: 1).
Row 3: Work as row 2.
Row 4: Work as row 1.
These 4 rows form the patt and are rep throughout.
Work a further 8 rows.
Dec 1 st at each end of next row and 4 foll 12th rows. 77 (81: 85: 89: 95: 103) sts.
Work straight until back measures 29 (30: 30: 30: 30: 30) cm from cast on edge, ending with a WS row.
Shape raglans
Cast off 4 (5: 5: 5: 5: 6) sts at beg of next 2 rows. 69 (71: 75: 79: 85: 91) sts.
Work 2 (2: 2: 2: 0: 0) rows.
Dec 1 st at each end of next row and every foll alt row until 35 (37: 39: 41: 43: 47) sts rem, and ending with a **RS** row.
Work 1 row. Cast off.

LEFT FRONT

Cast on 52 (54: 56: 60: 63: 67) sts using 4 ½ mm (US 7) needles.
Row 1 (RS): K0 (0: 0: 0: 1: 1), (P1, K1) to end.
Row 2: K1, (P1, K1) 5 (5: 5: 6: 6: 6) times, K1, (P1, K1) to last 0 (0: 0: 0: 1: 1) sts, P0 (0: 0: 0: 1: 1).
Row 3: P0 (0: 0: 0: 1: 1), (K1, P1) to last 12 (12: 12: 14: 14: 14) sts, (P1, K1) to end.
Row 4: K1, (P1, K1) 5 (5: 5: 6: 6: 6) times, K1, (K1, P1) to last 0 (0: 0: 0: 1: 1) sts, K0 (0: 0: 0: 1: 1).
These 4 rows set the stitches, i.e. the main part is worked in double moss st, with 11 (11: 11: 13: 13: 13) sts at front edge worked in moss st and these are separated with a st worked in rev st st, which is worked up the entire front.
Work a further 8 rows.

Dec 1 st at beg of next row and 4 foll 12th rows. 47 (49: 51: 55: 58: 62) sts.
Work straight until left front matches back to beg of raglan shaping, ending with a WS row.
Shape raglan
Cast off 4 (5: 5: 5: 5: 6) sts at beg of next row. 43 (44: 46: 50: 53: 56) sts.
Work 3 (3: 3: 3: 1: 1) rows, end with a WS row.
Dec 1 st at armhole edge on next row and every foll alt row until 34 (35: 37: 40: 41: 43) sts rem, ending with a RS row.
Work 1 row.

Shape front neck
Next row (RS): Dec 1 st, patt until there are 15 (15: 18: 18: 18: 18) sts on right needle and turn, leaving rem 18 (19: 18: 21: 22: 24) sts on a holder.
Cont to dec 1 at at armhole edge on every RS row and **at the same time** dec 1 st at neck edge on every foll row until 3 sts rem, ending with a RS row.
Work 1 row.
Next row (RS)(dec): K3tog.
Work 1 row. Fasten off.
Mark the position of first button 20 (20: 22: 24: 24: 26) rows down from neck edge (the second will be worked in the neck band).

RIGHT FRONT

Cast on 52 (54: 56: 60: 63: 67) sts using 4 ½ mm (US 7) needles.
Row 1 (RS): (K1, P1) to last 0 (0: 0: 0: 1: 1) sts, K0 (0: 0: 0: 1: 1).
Row 2: P0 (0: 0: 0: 1: 1), (K1, P1) to last 12 (12: 12: 14: 14: 14) sts, K1, (K1, P1) to last st, K1.
Row 3: (K1, P1) 6 (6: 6: 7: 7: 7) times, (P1, K1) to last 0 (0: 0: 0: 1: 1) sts, P0 (0: 0: 0: 1: 1).
Row 4: K0 (0: 0: 0: 1: 1), (P1, K1) to last 12 (12: 12: 14: 14: 14) sts, K1, (K1, P1) to last st, K1.
These 4 rows set the stitches, i.e. the main part is worked in double moss st, with 11 (11: 11: 13: 13: 13) sts at front edge worked in moss st and these are separated

with a st worked in rev st st which is worked up the entire front.

Work a further 8 rows.

Dec 1 st at end of next row and 4 foll 12th rows. 47 (49: 51: 55: 58: 62) sts.

Work straight until right front matches back to beg of raglan shaping, ending with a **RS** row.

Complete to match left front reversing all shapings and **at the same time** work a buttonhole to correspond with marker as folls:

Buttonhole row (RS): Patt 6 (6: 6: 7: 7:7) sts, cast off next 3 sts, patt to end.

Next row: Work to where 3 sts cast off, yrn 3 times, patt to end.

Next row: Patt across row, working into back of each of the 3 loops made on previous row.

SLEEVES (work both the same)

Cast on 59 (61: 63: 65: 67: 69) sts using 4 ½ mm (US 7) needles and work in double moss st as folls:

Row 1 (RS): K1, (P1, K1) to end.

Row 2: P1, (K1, P1) to end.

Row 3: Work as row 2.

Row 4: Work as row 1.

These 4 rows form the patt and are rep throughout.

Work a further 16 rows, ending with a WS row.

Dec 1 st at each end of next row and foll 20th row. 55 (57: 59: 61: 63: 65) sts.

Work straight until sleeve measures 32 (33: 34: 35: 36: 37) cm from cast on edge, ending with a WS row.

Shape raglans

Cast off 4 (5: 5: 5: 5: 6) sts at beg of next 2 rows. 47 (47: 49: 51: 53: 53) sts.

Work 2 rows.

Dec 1 st at each end of next row and every foll 4th row to 37 (37: 37: 39: 39: 37) sts, and then every foll alt row to 25 (25: 27: 27: 29: 29) sts, ending with a **RS** row.

Shape sleeve top

Left sleeve only

Cast off 8 (8: 9: 9: 9: 9) sts at beg of next row.

Dec 1 st at beg of next row.

Rep last 2 rows once more.

Cast off rem 7 (7: 7: 7: 9: 9) sts.

Right sleeve only

Work 1 row.

Cast off 8 (8: 9: 9: 9: 9) sts at beg and dec 1 st at end of next row.

Rep the last 2 rows once more.

Cast off rem 7 (7: 7: 7: 9: 9) sts.

MAKING UP

Press all pieces pieces using a warm iron over a damp cloth.

Join raglan seams using back stitch or mattress st if preferred.

Neck edging

With RS of right front facing and using 4 ½ mm (US 7) needles, slip 18 (19: 18: 21: 22: 24) sts from right front holder onto the right needle, rejoin yarn and pick 11 (11: 13: 13: 13: 13) sts across right front, 21 (21: 23: 23: 25: 25) sts across top of right sleeve, 33 (35: 37: 39: 43: 45) sts across back, 21 (21: 23: 23: 25: 25) sts across top of left sleeve and 11 (11: 13: 13: 13: 13) across left front to holder, and then work across sts on holder as folls: K to last 12 (12: 12: 14: 14: 14) sts, P1, patt to end. 133 (137: 145: 153: 163: 169) sts.

Place a marker on the needle at each end of the sleeve top sts.

Taking the markers up the knitting by slipping it from left to right needle, cont as folls:

Next row (WS): Patt 12 (12: 12: 14: 14: 14), K to last 12 (12: 12: 14: 14: 14), patt to end. The last row set the stitches, i.e. the main part is worked garter st, with 12 (12: 12: 14: 14: 14) sts at front edge worked in patt as already set.

Work 4 rows, ending with a WS row.

Change to 4mm (US 6) needles.

Next row (dec)(buttonhole): Patt 6 (6: 6: 7: 7: 7) sts, cast off next 3 sts, (patt to 4 sts before next marker, K2tog, K4, K2tog tbl) 4 times, patt to end. 125 (129: 137: 145: 155: 161) sts.

Work 3 rows completing buttonholes as given previously.

Next row (dec): (Patt to 4 sts before next marker, K2tog, K4, K2tog tbl) 4 times, patt to end. 117 (121: 129: 137: 147: 153) sts.

Work 1 row.

Next row (dec): (Patt to 4 sts before next marker, K2tog, K4, K2tog tbl) 4 times, patt to end. 109 (113: 121: 129: 139: 145) sts.

Cast off knitwise (on WS).

Join sides and sleeve seams.

Press seams.

Sew on buttons.

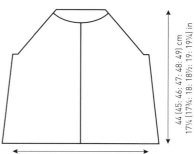

42.5 (45: 47.5: 49.5: 52.5: 57.5) cm
16¾ (17¾: 18¾: 19½: 20¾: 22¾) in

44 (45: 46: 47: 48: 49) cm
17¼ (17¾: 18: 18½: 19: 19¼) in

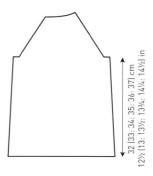

32 (33: 34: 35: 36: 37) cm
12½ (13: 13½: 13¾: 14¼: 14½) in

Recommendation

Suitable for the knitter with a little experience. Please see pages 12 & 13 for photographs.

	XS	S	M	L	XL	XXL	
To fit	**81**	**86**	**91**	**97**	**102**	**109**	**cm**
bust	32	34	36	38	40	43	in

Rowan Handknit cotton

14 15 16 17 18 20 x 50gm
Photographed in Burnt

Needles

1 pair 3¼ mm (no 10) (US 3) needles
1 pair 3¾ mm (no 9) (US 5) needles
1 pair 4 mm (no 8) (US 6) needles

Tension

20 sts and 28 rows to 10 cm measured over st st using 4 mm (US 6) needles.

Special abbreviation

MP = Make picot: cast on 1 st, cast off 1 st. (See information page for details)

Pattern note: When knitting fronts, it is advisable to join in new balls of yarn at side seam or armhole edge so that front opening edge remains neat and tidy as there are no front opening edgings added afterwards.

RUBY
BELTED CARDIGAN WITH GENEROUS BACK NECK

BACK

Cast on 87 (91: 97: 101: 107) sts using 3¾ mm (US 5) needles.
Work 14 rows in garter stitch, ending with a WS row.
Next row (RS) (dec): K2, K2tog, K to last 4 sts K2 tog tbl, K2.
85 (89: 95: 99: 105) sts.
Work a further 5 rows in garter stitch, ending with a WS row.
Dec as before on next row.
83 (87: 93: 97: 103) sts.
Work a further 3 rows in garter stitch, ending with a WS row.
Change to 4 mm (US 6) needles and, beg with a K row, cont in st st as folls:
Work 2 rows, ending with a WS row.
Next row (RS) (dec): K2, K2tog, K to last 4 sts, K2tog tbl, K2.
Work 5 rows.
Dec as before on next row and foll 6th row.
77 (81: 87: 91: 97) sts.
Work 9 (11: 13: 15: 17) rows, ending with a WS row.
Next row (RS) (inc): K2, M1, K to last 2 sts, M1, K2. 79 (83: 89: 93: 99) sts.
Work 9 rows.
Inc as before on next row, then on foll 10th row, then on every foll 8th row until there are 87 (91: 97: 101: 107) sts.
Cont straight until back measures 32.5 (33: 33.5: 34: 34.5) cm, ending with a WS row.
Shape raglans
Cast off 4 sts at beg of next 2 rows.
79 (83: 89: 93: 99) sts.
Work 2 rows.
Next row (RS) (dec): K2, K2tog, K to last 4 sts, K2 tog tbl, K2. 77 (81: 87: 91: 97) sts.
Work 3 rows.
Dec as before on next row and every foll 4th row until 57 (61: 71: 73: 83) sts rem.
Work 1 row.
Dec as before on next row and every foll alt row until 49 (51: 51: 53: 53) sts rem.
Work 1 row, ending with a WS row.
Cast off.

LEFT FRONT

Cast on 54 (56: 59: 61: 64) sts using 3¾ mm (US 5) needles.
Row 1: Knit.
Row 2: MP, K to end.
Row 3 & 4: Knit.
Working a picot as set on 2nd and every foll 4th row up the entire front opening edge, cont as folls:
Work 10 rows, ending with a WS row.
Next row (RS) (dec): K2, K2tog, K to end.
53 (55: 58: 60: 63) sts.
Work 5 rows, ending with a WS row.
Dec as before on next row.
52 (54: 57: 59: 62) sts.
Work 3 rows, ending with a WS row.
Change to 4 mm (US 6) needles and cont in patt as folls:
Next row (RS): Knit.
Next row: MP, K until 11 sts on right needle, P to end.
Next row (RS) (dec): K2, K2tog, K to end.
Working 11 sts at centre in garter st with picot edging as set, and rem sts in st st, cont as folls:
Work 5 rows.
Dec as before on next row and foll 6th row.
49 (51: 54: 56: 59) sts.
Work 9 (11: 13: 15: 17) rows, ending with a WS row.
Next row (RS) (inc): K2, M1, K to end.
Work 9 rows.
Inc as before on next row, then on foll 10th row, then on every foll 8th row until there are 54 (56: 59: 61: 64) sts.
Cont straight until left front matches back to beg of armhole shaping, ending with a WS row.
Shape raglan
Cast off 4 sts at beg of next row.
50 (52: 55: 57: 60) sts.
Work 3 rows.
Next row (RS) (dec): K2, K2tog, K to end.
49 (51: 54: 56: 59)
Work 3 rows.
Dec as before on next row and every foll 4th row until 39 (41: 46: 47: 52) sts rem.
Work 1 row.

Dec as before on next row and every foll alt row until 35 (36: 36: 37: 37) sts rem.
Work 1 row.
Break yarn and leave sts on a spare needle.

RIGHT FRONT
Cast on 54 (56: 59: 61: 64) sts using 3¾ mm (US 5) needles.
Row 1: MP, K to end.
Row 2: Knit.
Row 3 & 4: Knit.
Working a picot as set on next and every foll 4th row up the entire front opening edge, cont as folls:
Work 10 rows, ending with a WS row.
Next row (RS) (dec): K to last 4 sts, K2tog tbl, K2. 53 (55: 58: 60: 63) sts.
Work 5 rows, ending with a WS row.
Dec as before on next row.
52 (54: 57: 59: 62) sts.
Work 3 rows, ending with a WS row.
Change to 4 mm (US 6) needles and cont in patt, complete as given for left front reversing shapings.
Do not break yarn.
Leave yarn attached for collar.
Leave sts on a spare needle.

SLEEVES (both alike)
Lower edging (knitted from side to side)
Cast on 14 (15: 16: 17: 18) sts using 3¾ mm (US 5) needles.
Knit 2 rows.
Shape side edge
Next row (RS): MP, K until there are 6 (7: 8: 9: 10) sts on right needle, wrap next stitch (by slipping next st to right needle, taking yarn to opposite side of work between needles and then slipping same st back onto left needle – when working back across sts, work the wrapped loop tog with the wrapped st), turn and K to end.
Next row: MP, K until 10 (11: 12: 13: 14) sts on right needle, wrap next stitch, turn and K to end.
Keeping picot edging correct as set, work a further 80 (88: 96: 104: 112) rows, ending with a WS row.
Shape side edge
Next row: MP, K until 10 (11: 12: 13: 14) sts on right needle, wrap next stitch, turn and K to end.
Next row: MP, K until 6 (7: 8: 9: 10) sts on right needle, wrap next stitch, turn and K to end.
Knit 2 rows.
Cast off, but do not break yarn.

Upper sleeve
With RS of lower edging facing and using 4 mm (US 6) needles, pick up and knit 49 (53: 57: 61: 65) sts evenly along the top (straight) edge of lower edging and purl 1 row, ending with a WS row.
Beg with a K row, cont in st st as folls:
Work 4 rows.
Next row (RS) (dec): K2, K2tog, K to last 4 sts, K2tog tbl, K2.
47 (51: 55: 59: 63) sts.
Work 3 rows, ending with a WS row.
Dec as before on next row and foll 4th row.
43 (47: 51: 55: 59) sts.
Work 13 rows, ending with a WS row.
Next row (RS)(inc): K2, M1, K to last 2 sts, M1, K2. 45 (49: 53: 57: 61) sts.
Work 9 rows, ending with a WS row.
Inc as before on next row, then on 2 foll 10th rows, then on every foll 8th row until there are 59 (63: 67: 71: 75) sts.
Cont until sleeve measures 42 (43: 44: 45: 46) cm, ending with a WS row.
Shape raglan
Cast off 4 sts at beg of next 2 rows.
51 (55: 59: 63: 67) sts.
Work 2 rows.
Next row (RS) (dec): K2, K2tog, K to last 4 sts, K2tog tbl, K2.
Work 3 rows.
Dec as before on next row and every foll 4th row until 35 (39: 45: 47: 53) sts rem.
Work 1 row.
Dec as before on next row and every foll alt row until 15 (17: 17: 19: 19) sts rem.
Work 1 row. Cast off.

MAKING UP
Press all pieces using a warm iron over a damp cloth.
Join raglan seams using back stitch or mattress stitch if preferred.
Collar
With RS facing and using 3¾ mm (US 5) needles, work across 35 (36: 36: 37: 37) sts from right front as folls: (working picot where applicable) K11 (12: 12: 11: 11) sts on right needle, (P1, K1) to last 2 sts, P2tog, pick up and knit 13 (15: 15: 17: 17) across top of right sleeve, 47 (49: 49: 51: 51) sts across back, 13 (15: 15: 17: 17) sts across top of left sleeve, then work across 35 (36: 36: 37: 37) sts from left front as folls: P2tog, (K1, P1)

to last 11 (12: 12: 11: 11) sts, K11 (12: 12: 11: 11). 141 (149: 149: 157: 157) sts.
Next row (WS of garment, RS of collar): K11, rib to last 11 sts, K11.
Cont as set until collar measures 13 (14: 14: 15: 15) cm.
Cast off in pattern. Join side and sleeve seams.
Belt
Using 3¼ mm (US 3) needles, work picot caston as folls:
Cast on 4 sts, cast off 1 st, slip loop on right needle onto left needle, *cast on 3 sts, cast off 1 st, slip loop on right needle onto left needle, rep from * until 12 sts have been cast-on.
Row 1 (RS): MP, K to last 2 sts, inc in next st, K1. 13 sts.
Row 2: MP, K to last 2 sts, K2tog tbl. 12 sts.
Rep these 2 rows until belt measures 140 cm.
Work picot cast-off as folls: Cast off 2 sts, *slip st on right needle onto left needle, cast on 2 sts, cast off 4 sts, rep from * to end.

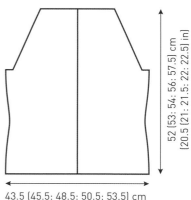

43.5 (45.5: 48.5: 50.5: 53.5) cm
(17 (18: 19: 20: 21) in)

52 (53: 54: 56: 57.5) cm
(20.5 (21: 21.5: 22: 22.5) in)

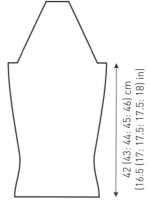

42 (43: 44: 45: 46) cm
(16.5 (17: 17.5: 17.5: 18) in)

Recommendation
Suitable for the knitter with a little experienced
Please see pages 14 & 15 for photographs.

	XS	S	M	L	XL	XXL	
To fit	**81**	**86**	**91**	**97**	**102**	**109**	cm
bust	32	34	36	38	40	43	in

Rowan Handknit Cotton
8 8 9 10 11 12 x 50gm
Photographed in Turkish Plum

Buttom – 8 small

Needles
1 pair 3 ¼mm (no 10) (US 3) needles
1 pair 3 ¾mm (no 9) (US 5) needles
1 pair 4mm (no 8) (US 6) needles
1 4.00 mm (US G6) crochet hook

Tension
20 sts and 28 rows to 10cm measured over
pattern using 4mm (US 6) needles

Special abbreviation:
MP = Make picot: cast on 1 st, cast off 1 st.
(See information page for details)
Tw2L = Knit into back of 2nd stitch, then knit
into front of the first stitch.

WILLOW
TUNIC WITH DEEP SCOOPED NECKLINE

BACK
Lower back edging
Cast on 16 (16: 16: 18: 18: 20) sts using
3 ¾mm (US 5) needles and work as folls:
Row 1 (RS): MP, P to end.
Row 2: Knit.
Row 3: MP, K to end.
Row 4: P1, * yrn, P2tog, rep from * to last st, P1.
Row 5: MP, P to end.
Row 6: Knit.
Row 7: MP, K to end.
Row 8: Purl.
Rep last 8 rows a further 14 (15: 16: 17: 18: 19)
times, then rows 1 – 6 again, ending with a
WS row.
Cast off, but do not break yarn.

UPPER BACK
With RS facing and using 4 mm (US 6)
needles, pick up and knit 82 (88: 92: 98:
102: 110) sts along straight edge of border
and cont as folls:
Next row (WS)(foundation row): K4 (7: 9: 12:
2: 6), P2, *K10, P2, rep from * to last 4 (7: 9:
12: 2: 6) sts, K4 (7: 9: 12: 2: 6).
This row sets the sts for patt.
Cont in patt from chart, rep the 20 patt rep
throughout, and **at the same time,** work
shapings as folls:
Work 4 rows, ending with a WS row.
Dec 1 st at each end of next row and 3 foll
6th rows. 74 (80: 84: 90: 94: 102) sts.
Work 15 rows in patt as set, ending with a WS row.
Inc 1 st at each end of next row and 5 foll
8th rows.
86 (92: 96: 102: 106: 114) sts.
Cont straight until back measures 33 (33: 34:
34: 34: 34) cm from pick-up row, ending with
a WS row.
Shape armholes
Cast off 5 (5: 5: 6: 6: 6) sts at beg of next 2 rows.
76 (82: 86: 90: 94: 102) sts.
Dec 1 st at each end of next 5 (5: 5: 5: 7: 7)
rows, then on 2 (3: 4: 4: 3: 5) foll alt rows,
then on foll 4th row.
60 (64: 66: 70: 72: 76) sts.

Cont straight until armhole measures
18 (19: 19: 20: 21: 22) cm, ending with
a WS row.
Shape shoulders and back neck
Cast off 4 (4: 4: 5: 5: 5) sts at beg of next 2 rows.
Next row (RS): Cast off 4 (4: 4: 4: 4: 5) sts,
patt until there are 7 (8: 8: 8: 8: 8) sts on RH
needle and turn, leaving rem sts on a holder.
Work each side of neck separately.
Cast off 4 sts at beg of next row.
Cast off rem 3 (4: 4: 4: 4: 4) sts.
With RS facing, rejoin yarn to rem sts, cast off
centre 30 (32: 34: 36: 38: 40) sts, patt to end.
Complete to match first side, reversing shapings.

FRONT
Work as given for back until front is 28 (26:
28: 28: 28: 28) rows shorter than back to
beg of armhole shaping, 82 (88: 92: 98: 102:
110) sts on needle, and ending with a WS row.
Now cont shaping side and armhole as given
for back and **at the same time** divide and
shape front neck as folls:
Shape front neck
Keeping side shaping correct, work until
34 (36: 38: 40: 42: 46) sts on right needle
and turn, leaving rem sts on a holder.
Work each side of neck separately.
Dec 1 st at neck edge on next 4 rows and
3 (3: 4: 4: 5: 6) foll alt rows ending with
a RS row.
Work 3 rows.
Dec 1 st at neck edge on next row and foll
6th row, ending with a **RS** row.
Now cont shaping neck edge as folls, but
at the same time when front matches back to
beg of armhole shaping, shape armhole as
given for back.
Work 7 rows.
Dec 1 st at neck edge on next row, then on
foll 10th row and then on foll 12th row, (by
which time the armhole shaping will now be
completed.
11 (12: 12: 13: 13: 14) sts.
Work straight until front matches back to
shoulder shaping, ending with a WS row.

Back & Front

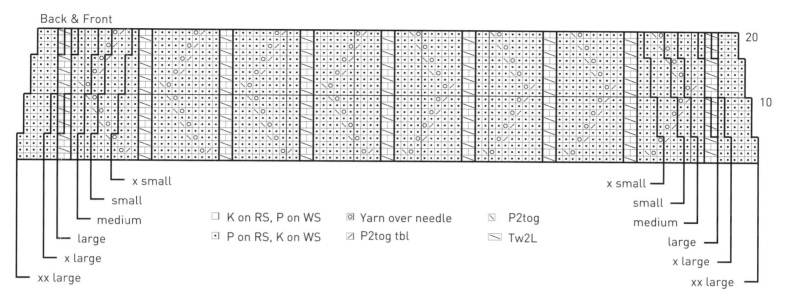

— x small			
— small			
— medium			
— large			
— x large			
— xx large			

☐ K on RS, P on WS   ☑ Yarn over needle   ◲ P2tog

⊡ P on RS, K on WS   ☑ P2tog tbl   ◿ Tw2L

x small —
small —
medium —
large —
x large —
xx large —

Shape shoulder
Cast off 4 (4: 4: 5: 5: 5) at beg of next row
and 4 (4: 4: 4: 4: 5) sts at beg of foll alt row.
Work 1 row.
Cast off rem 3 (4: 4: 4: 4: 4) sts.
With RS facing rejoin yarn to rem sts, cast off
centre 14 (16: 16: 18: 18: 18) sts, patt to
end. 34 (36: 38: 40: 42: 46) sts.
Complete to match first side reversing
shaping.

CAP SLEEVES (work both the same)
Cast on 94 (102: 102: 106: 110: 114) sts
using 3 ¼ mm (US 3) needles.
Row 1 (RS): P2, (K2, P2) to end.
Row 2: K2, (P2, K2) to end.
These 2 row form the rib and are repeated
throughout.
Work a further 4 (4: 4: 4: 6: 6) rows, ending
with a WS row.
Cast off 6 (10: 10: 10: 12: 12) sts at beg of
next 2 rows. 82 (82: 82: 86: 86: 90) sts.
Cast off 6 (6: 6: 8: 8: 10) sts at beg of next
2 rows. 70 sts.
Cast off 6 sts at beg of next 8 rows.
Cast off rem 22 sts.

MAKING UP
Press back and front using a warm iron over
a damp cloth.

Join right shoulder seam using backstitch or
mattress st if preferred.
Neck edging
With RS of front facing and using
3 ¼ mm (US 3) needles pick and knit
66 (68: 70: 72: 74: 76) sts from left
shoulder down to cast off sts at centre
front, 14 (16: 16: 18: 18: 18) sts across
centre front, 66 (68: 70: 72: 74: 76) sts
up right front to shoulder and 38 (40: 42:
44: 46: 48) sts across back.
184 (192: 198: 206: 212: 218) sts.
Next row (WS): P0 (0: 2: 2: 0: 2), (K2, P2)
to end.
Next row: (K2, P2) to last 0 (0: 2: 2: 0: 2) sts,
K0 (0: 2: 2: 0: 2).
These 2 rows set the sts for the rib.
Work a further 5 rows in rib, ending with
a WS row.
Cast off in rib.
Join left shoulder and neck edging seam.
Sew cap sleeve into armhole.
Join side and sleeve seams, leaving side
seams open at border edges.
Using 4 mm (US G6) crochet hook, make
4 button loops along each side of front
border edge.
Sew on buttons to correspond with button
loops.

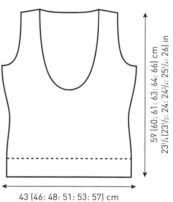

59 (60: 61: 63: 64: 66) cm
23¼ (23½: 24: 24¾: 25¼: 26) in

43 (46: 48: 51: 53: 57) cm
17 (18: 19: 20: 21: 22½) in

GEORGIE
RELAXED HOODED CARDIGAN

Recommendation
Suitable for the knitter with a little experience.
Please see pages 19, 42 & 43 for photographs.

	XS	S	M	L	XL	XXL	
To fit	**81**	**86**	**91**	**97**	**102**	**109**	cm
bust	32	34	36	38	40	43	in

Rowan Classic Pima Cotton DK
15 16 17 18 19 20 x50gm

Photographed in Peppercorn

Needles
1 pair 3 ¾mm (no 9) (US 5) needles

Tension
23 sts and 30 rows to 10 cm measured over
stocking stitch using 3 ¾mm (US 5) needles.

BACK
Cast on 111 (117: 123: 129: 135: 145) sts
using 3 ¾mm (US 5) needles.
Beg with a K row, work in st st as folls:
Work 20 rows.
Row 21 (dec) (RS): K2, K2tog, K to last 4 sts,
K2tog tbl, K2.
Work 15 rows.
Dec 1 st as before at each end of next and
every foll 16th row until 97 (103: 109: 115:
121: 131) sts rem.
Work straight until back measures 54 (54: 55:
55: 55: 55) cm, ending with a WS row.
Shape armholes
Cast off 4 (5: 5: 6: 6: 7) sts at beg of next
2 rows.
89 (93: 99: 103: 109: 117) sts.
Dec 1 st at each end of next 3 (3: 5: 5: 7: 9)
rows, then on foll 2 (3: 3: 4: 4: 5) alt rows,
then on foll 4th row.
77 (79: 81: 83: 85: 87) sts.
Work straight until armhole measures
18 (19: 19: 20: 21: 22) cm, ending with
a WS row.
Shape shoulders and back neck
Cast off 6 sts at beg of next 2 rows.
65 (67: 69: 71: 73: 75) sts.
Next row (RS): Cast off 6 sts, K until there are
9 sts on right needle and turn, leaving rem sts
on a holder.
Work each side of neck separately.
Cast off 4 sts at beg of next row.
Cast off rem 5 sts.
With RS facing rejoin yarn to rem sts, cast off
centre 35 (37: 39: 41: 43: 45) sts, K to end.
Complete to match first side rev shaping.

Pattern note: When knitting fronts, it is
advisable to join in new balls of yarn at side
seam or armhole edge so that front opening
edge remains neat and tidy as there are no
front opening edgings added afterwards.

LEFT FRONT
Cast on 96 (99: 102: 105: 108: 113) sts using
3 ¾mm (US 5) needles and work as folls:

Row 1 (RS): Knit.
Row 2: K2, P to end.
Working 2 sts at front opening edge in
garter st throughout and rem sts in st
st cont as folls:
Work 18 rows.
Row 21 (dec) (RS): K2, K2tog, K to end.
Work 15 rows.
Dec 1 st as before at beg of next and every
foll 16th row until 89 (92: 95: 98: 101: 106)
sts rem.
Work straight until left front matches back
to beg of armhole shaping, ending with a
WS row.
Shape armhole
Cast off 4 (5: 5: 6: 6: 7) sts at beg of next row.
85 (87: 90: 92: 95: 99) sts.
Work 1 row.
Dec 1 st at armhole edge of next 3 (3: 5: 5: 7:
9) rows, then on foll 2 (3: 3: 4: 4: 5) alt rows,
then on foll 4th row.
79 (80: 81: 82: 83: 84) sts.
Work straight until left front matches back
to start of shoulder shaping, ending with
a WS row.
Shape shoulder
Cast off 6 sts at beg of next and foll alt row,
then 5 sts at beg of foll alt row.
62 (63: 64: 65: 66: 67) sts.
Work 1 row, ending with a WS row.
Shape hood
Keeping sts correct as set, cast on 21 (22: 23:
24: 25: 26) sts at beg of next row.
83 (85: 87: 89: 91: 93) sts.
Cont straight until work measures 13 (13: 14:
14: 15: 15) cm from hood cast-on sts, ending
with a WS row.
Working all hood decreases in same way
as side seam decreases, dec 1 st at beg
of next and foll 12th row, then on foll 10th
row, then on foll 8th row, then on foll 6th
row, then on 3 foll 4th rows, then on foll
2 alt rows. 73 (75: 77: 79: 81: 83) sts.
Work 1 row, ending with a WS row.
Next row (dec) (RS): K2, K2tog, K to end.
Next row: K2, P to last 4 sts, P2tog, P2.

Rep last 2 rows twice more.
67 (69: 71: 73: 75: 77) sts.
Cast off 4 sts at beg of next row, 6 sts at beg of foll alt row, 10 sts at beg of foll alt row, then 12 sts at beg of foll alt row.
Work 1 row, ending with a WS row.
Leave rem 35 (37: 39: 41: 43: 45) sts on a holder.

RIGHT FRONT

Cast on 96 (99: 102: 105: 108: 113) sts using 3 ¾mm (US 5) needles and work as folls:
Row 1 (RS): Knit.
Row 2: P to last 2 sts, K2.
Working 2 sts at front opening edge in garter st throughout and rem sts in st st cont as folls:
Work 18 rows.
Row 21 (dec) (RS): K to last 4 sts, K2tog tbl, K2.
Complete to match left front, reversing shapings.

SLEEVES (both alike)
Lower sleeve
Cast on 53 (55: 57: 59: 61: 63) sts using 3 ¾mm (US 5) needles.

Beg with a K row cont in st st as folls:
Work 20 rows, ending with a WS row.
Row 21(inc) (RS): K3, M1, K to last 3 sts, M1, K3. 55 (57: 59: 61: 63: 65) sts.
Work 13 (13: 13: 13: 13: 15) rows.
Inc 1 st as before at each end of next row.
57 (59: 61: 63: 65: 67) sts.
Work 11 (11: 11: 11: 11: 9) rows, ending with a WS row.
Cast off.

Main section
With **WS** of lower sleeve facing (so that a ridge is created on RS of work) and using 3 ¾mm (US 5) needles, pick up and knit 57 (59: 61: 63: 65: 67) sts across cast off edge of lower sleeve.
Beg with a K row cont in st st as folls:
Work 2 (2: 2: 2: 2: 4) rows.
Inc 1 st as before at each end of next and every foll 12th (14th: 14th: 14th: 14th: 14th) row to 73 (65: 69: 75: 79: 83) sts, then on 0 (5: 4: 2: 1: 0) foll 12th rows.
73 (75: 77: 79: 81: 83) sts.
Work straight until sleeve measures 49 (50: 51: 52: 53: 54) cm **from lower sleeve cast-on edge,** ending with a WS row.

Shape sleeve top
Cast off 4 (5: 5: 6: 6: 7) sts at beg of next 2 rows.
65 (65: 67: 67: 69: 69) sts.
Dec 1 st at each end of next 3 rows, then on foll alt row, then on 4 (5: 5: 6: 6: 7) foll 4th rows. 49 (47: 49: 47: 49: 47) sts.
Work 1 row.
Dec 1 st at each end of next and foll 4 (3: 4: 3: 4: 3) alt rows, then on foll 3 rows, ending with a WS row. 33 sts.
Cast off 3 sts at beg of next 2 rows.
Cast off rem 27 sts.

MAKING UP
Pin out pieces and press carefully following instructions on ball band.
Join both shoulder seams using back stitch, or mattress stitch if preferred.
Join top seam of hood by grafting together the 2 sets of sts left on holders. Join shaped cast-off and row-end edges of hood to form back seam of hood, then sew cast-on edge of hood to back neck edge, positioning hood seam at centre back neck. Join side seams. Join sleeve seams. Set in sleeves.

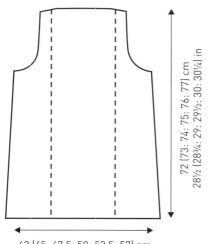

42 (45: 47.5: 50: 52.5: 57) cm
16½ (17¾: 18¾: 19¾: 20¾: 22½) in

72 (73: 74: 75: 76: 77) cm
28½ (28¾: 29: 29½: 30: 30¼) in

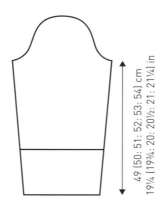

49 (50: 51: 52: 53: 54) cm
19¼ (19¾: 20: 20½: 21: 21¼) in

DOLLY
CARDIGAN WITH MOSS STITCH FLOUNCE & CONTRASTING TRIMS

Recommendation
Suitable for the knitter with a little experience.
Please see page 20 for photograph.

	XS	S	M	L	XL	XXL	
To fit	**81**	**86**	**91**	**97**	**102**	**107**	cm
bust	32	34	36	38	40	42	in

Rowan Milk Cotton Fine
Main colour

8	9	9	10	11	12	x 50gm

Contrast

1	1	1	1	1	1	x 50gm

Photographed in Pastille & Tutti Frutti

Buttons – 5 large & 2 small

Needles
1 pair 2 ¼ mm (no 13) (US 1) needles
1 pair 2 ¾ mm (no 12) (US 2) needles

Tension
29 sts and 38 rows to 10 cm measured over
stocking stitch using 2 ¾ mm (US 2) needles.

Pattern note: When knitting fronts, it is
advisable to join in new balls of yarn at side
seam or armhole edge so that front opening
edge remains neat and tidy as there are no
front opening edgings added afterwards.

BACK
Cast on 171 (185: 195: 207: 221: 241) sts
using 2 ¾ mm (US 2) needles and **main
colour.**
Work lower frill as folls:
Row 1 (RS): K1, (P1, K1) to end.
Row 2: Work as row 1.
These 2 rows form moss st.
Cont in moss st until work measures 8 (8: 9:
9: 10: 10) cm, ending with a WS row.
**Change to 2 ¼ mm (US 1) needles and cont
in st st as folls:**
Next row (dec) (RS): K0 (0: 0: 1: 0: 0) (K1,
K3tog, K1) 34 (37: 39: 41: 44: 48) times,
K1 (0: 0: 1: 1: 1).
103 (111: 117: 125: 133: 145) sts.
Work 5 rows.
Change to 2 ¾ mm (US 2) needles.
Work 6 rows, ending with a WS row.
Next row (RS) (inc): K2, M1, K to last 2 sts,
M1, K2.
105 (113: 119: 127: 135: 147) sts.
Work 9 rows.
Inc 1 st as before at each end of next
and every foll 10th row until there are
117 (125: 131: 139: 147: 159) sts.
Work straight until back measures 23 (24:
25: 25: 25: 26: 26) cm **from top of moss st frill,**
ending with a WS row.
Shape armholes
Cast off 5 (5: 5: 6: 6: 6) sts at beg of next
2 rows.
107 (115: 121: 127: 135: 147) sts.
Dec 1 st at each end of next 5 (5: 5: 5: 5: 9)
rows, then on foll 2 (4: 5: 5: 7: 7) alt rows,
and then on foll 4th row.
91 (95: 99: 105: 109: 113) sts.
Work straight until armhole measures 18 (19:
20: 20: 21: 22) cm, ending with a WS row.
Shape shoulders and back neck
Cast off 7 (7: 8: 8: 9: 9) sts at beg of next
2 rows. 77 (81: 83: 89: 91: 95) sts.
Next row (RS): Cast off 7 (7: 8: 8: 9: 9) sts,
K until there are 11 (12: 11: 13: 12: 13) sts
on right needle and turn, leaving rem sts on
a holder.

Work each side of neck separately.
Cast off 4 sts at beg of next row.
Cast off rem 7 (8: 7: 9: 8: 9) sts.
With RS facing rejoin yarn to rem sts, cast off
centre 41 (43: 45: 47: 49: 51) sts, K to end.
Complete to match first side, reversing
shapings.

LEFT FRONT
Cast on 97 (103: 108: 116: 122: 132) sts
using 2 ¾ mm (US 2) needles and **main
colour.**
Work lower frill as folls:
Row 1 (RS): *K1, P1; rep from * to last 1 (1:
0: 0: 0: 0) st, K1 (1: 0: 0: 0: 0).
Row 2: K1 (1: 0: 0: 0: 0), *P1, K1; rep from
* to end.
These 2 rows form moss st.
Cont in moss st until work measures 8 (8: 9:
9: 10: 10) cm, ending with a WS row.
**Change to 2 ¼ mm (US 1) needles and cont
as folls:**
Next row (dec) (RS): K1 (1: 1: 0: 1: 1), (K1,
K3tog, K1) 17 (18: 19: 21: 22: 24) times, K0
(1: 1: 0: 0: 0), moss st 11 sts (to form front
band).
63 (67: 70: 74: 78: 84) sts.
Next row: Moss st 11 sts, P to end.
Working 11 sts at front opening edge in moss
stitch and all other sts in st st, cont as folls:
Work 4 rows.
Change to 2 ¾ mm (US 2) needles
Work 6 rows, ending with a WS row.
Next row (RS) (inc): K2, M1, patt to end.
64 (68: 71: 75: 79: 85) sts.
Work 9 rows.
Inc 1 st as before at beg of next and every
foll 10th row until there are 70 (74: 77:
81: 85: 91) sts.
Work straight until left front matches back
to beg of armhole shaping, ending with
a WS row.
Shape armhole
Cast off 5 (5: 5: 6: 6: 6) sts at beg of next
row. 65 (69: 72: 75: 79: 85) sts.
Work 1 row.

Dec 1 st at armhole edge on next 5 (5: 5: 5: 5: 9) rows, then on foll 2 (4: 5: 5: 7: 7) alt rows, and then on foll 4th row. 57 (59: 61: 64: 66: 68) sts.
Work straight until front is 20 (22: 24: 24: 26: 26) rows shorter than back to beg of shoulder shaping, ending with a WS row.

Shape front neck
Next row (RS): K32 (35: 37: 40: 42: 43) and turn, leaving rem 25 (24: 24: 24: 24: 25) sts on a holder for neckband.
Dec 1 st at neck edge on next 6 (8: 8: 10: 10: 10) rows, then on 4 (4: 5: 4: 5: 5) foll alt rows, and then on foll 4th row.
21 (22: 23: 25: 26: 27) sts.
Work 1 row, ending with a WS row.

Shape shoulder
Cast off 7 (7: 8: 8: 9: 9) sts at beg of next and foll alt row.
Work 1 row.
Cast off rem 7 (8: 7: 9: 8: 9) sts.
Mark position for 5 buttons along left front opening edge · first to come in 3rd row after frill, last to come 2 rows down from neck edge and rem 3 buttons spaced evenly between.

RIGHT FRONT
Cast on 97 (103: 108: 116: 122: 132) sts using 2 ¾ mm (US 2) needles and **main colour.**
Work lower frill as folls:
Row 1 (RS): K1 (1: 0: 0: 0: 0), *P1, K1; rep from * to end.
Row 2: *K1, P1; rep from * to last 1 (1: 0: 0: 0: 0) st, K1 (1: 0: 0: 0: 0).
These 2 rows form moss st.
Cont in moss st until work measures 8 (8: 9: 9: 10: 10) cm, ending with a WS row.
Change to 2 ¼ mm (US 1) needles and cont as folls:
Next row (dec) (RS): Moss st 11 sts (to form front band), K1 (1: 1: 0: 1: 1), (K1, K3tog, K1) 17 (18: 19: 21: 22: 24) times, K0 (1: 1: 0: 0: 0). 63 (67: 70: 74: 78: 84) sts.
Next row: P to last 11 sts, moss st 11 sts.
Working 11 sts at centre front in moss stitch and rem sts in st st, cont as folls:
Next row (buttonhole row) (RS): Moss st 4 sts, cast off 4 sts (to make a buttonhole – cast on 4 sts over these cast-off sts on next row), patt to end.
Work 3 rows.

Change to 2 ¾ mm (US 2) needles.
Work 6 rows, ending with a WS row.
Next row(inc) (RS): Patt to last 2 sts, M1, K2.
64 (68: 71: 75: 79: 85) sts.
Complete to match left front, reversing shapings and working a further 4 buttonholes as before to correspond with positions marked for buttons.

LEFT SLEEVE
Sleeve front
Cast on 49 (49: 51: 51: 55: 55) sts using 2 ¼ mm (US 1) needles and **contrast colour.**
Break off contrast colour, join in **main colour** and cont as folls:
Next row (RS): Knit.
Work 11 (11: 11: 13: 13: 13) rows in moss st as given for back, ending with a WS row.
Break yarn and leave sts on a spare needle.
Sleeve back
Cast on 29 (31: 33: 35: 35: 37) sts using 2 ¼ mm (US 1) needles and contrast colour.
Break off **contrast colour,** join in **main colour** and cont as folls:
Next row (RS): Knit.
Work 11 (11: 11: 13: 13: 13) rows in moss st as given for back, ending with a WS row.
Do not break yarn.
Join sleeve front & back
Next row (RS): K to last 7 sts of sleeve back, now holding sleeve back behind sleeve front and taking 1 st from each needle together, K tog next st of sleeve back with first st of sleeve front, (K tog next st of sleeve back with next st of sleeve front) 6 times, K rem sts of sleeve front.
71 (73: 77: 79: 83: 85) sts.
**Next row: Purl.
Change to 2 ¾ mm (US 2) needles and, beg with a K row, cont in st st as folls:
Work 2 rows.
Next row (inc) (RS): K2, M1, K to last 2 sts, M1, K2.
73 (75: 79: 81: 85: 87) sts.
Work 9 (9: 9: 9: 11: 9) rows.
Inc 1 st as before at each end of next and 6 (5: 3: 7: 0: 0) foll 10th rows, then on every foll 12th row until there are 91 (93: 97: 101: 103: 105) sts.
Work straight until sleeve measures 31 (32: 33: 34: 35: 36) cm, ending with a WS row.

Shape sleeve top
Cast off 5 (5: 5: 6: 6: 6) sts at beg of next 2 rows.
81 (83: 87: 89: 91: 93) sts.
Dec 1 st at each end of next 3 rows, then on foll 2 alt rows, and then on every foll 4th row until 61 (61: 63: 65: 67: 65) sts rem, ending with a **RS** row.
Work 1 row.
Dec 1 st at each end of next and foll 5 (5: 4: 4: 5: 4) alt rows, then on every foll row until 35 (35: 35: 37: 37: 41) sts rem, ending with a WS row.
Cast off 4 sts at beg of next 2 rows.
Cast off rem 27 (27: 27: 29: 29: 33) sts.

RIGHT SLEEVE
Sleeve back
Cast on 29 (31: 33: 35: 35: 37) sts using 2 ¼ mm (US 1) needles and **contrast colour.**
Break off contrast colour, join in main colour and cont as folls:
Next row (RS): Knit.
Work 11 (11: 11: 13: 13: 13) rows in moss st as given for back, ending with a WS row.
Break yarn and leave sts on a spare needle.
Sleeve front
Cast on 49 (49: 51: 51: 55: 55) sts using 2 ¼ mm (US 1) needles and **contrast colour.**
Break off contrast colour, join in **main colour** and cont as folls:
Next row (RS): Knit.
Work 11 (11: 11: 13: 13: 13) rows in moss st as given for back, ending with a WS row.
Do not break yarn.

Join sleeve front & back
Next row (RS): K to last 7 sts of sleeve front, now holding sleeve back **behind** sleeve front and taking 1 st from each needle together, K tog next st of sleeve front with first st of sleeve back, (K tog next st of sleeve front with next st of sleeve back) 6 times, K rem sts of sleeve back.
71 (73: 77: 79: 83: 85) sts.
Complete as given for left sleeve from **.

MAKING UP
Press all pieces using a warm iron over a damp cloth.
Join both shoulder seams using back stitch or mattress st if preferred.

Neck edging

With RS of right front facing, using 2 ¼ mm
(US 1) needles and **main colour,** slip 25 (24:
24: 24: 24: 25) sts from right front holder
onto right needle, rejoin yarn and pick up
and knit 24 (26: 28: 28: 30: 30) sts up right
side of neck, 49 (51: 53: 55: 57: 59) sts from
back, and 24 (26: 28: 28: 30: 30) sts down
left side of neck, then patt across 25 (24: 24:
24: 24: 25) sts on left front holder.
147 (151: 157: 159: 165: 169) sts.
Keeping moss st correct as set by front
opening edge sts, work 9 rows in moss st
across all sts, ending with a WS row.
Cast off in moss st.
Join sleeve and side seams.
Set sleeves into armholes.
Using **contrast colour,** sew on buttons to
correspond with buttonholes, attaching
smaller buttons to sleev

49 (51: 54: 54: 57: 58) cm
19¼ (20: 21¼: 21¼: 22½: 22¾) in

40.5 (43: 45: 48: 50.5 55) cm
16 (17: 18: 19: 20: 21½) in

31 (32: 33: 34: 35: 36) cm
12¼ (12½: 13: 13½: 13¾: 14¼) in

Recommendation

Suitable for average ability.
Please see pages 21, 41 & 52 for photographs.

Rowan Handknit Cotton DK

2 x 50gm
Photographed in Pesto, Double Choc & Antique

Needles

4 mm (US G6) hook
3.25 mm (US D3)

Finished size: One size

Special abbreviations

Tr2tog (dec): *Wrap the yarn round the hook, insert the hook into top of next tr, wrap the yarn, draw a loop through, wrap the yarn and draw through 2 of the loops on hook (2 loops left on the hook), rep from *, (3 loops left on the hook), wrap the yarn and draw through all the loops on hook.

5 treble bobble = tr5tog : Wrap the yarn round the hook, insert the hook into next st, wrap the yarn, draw a loop through, wrap the yarn and draw through 2 of the loops on the hook (2 loops left on the hook) *wrap the yarn round the hook, insert the hook into the same st, wrap the yarn, draw a loop through, wrap the yarn and draw through 2 of the loops on the hook (3 loops left on the hook); rep from * 3 times more (6 loops on hook), wrap the yarn over the hook and draw through all the loops on the hook.

PEACHES
SLOUCHY CROCHET BERET

BERET

Using 4 mm (US G6) hook, make 4 ch, ss into first ch to form a ring.

Round 1: 1ch, work 9dc into ring, ss into 1st st. 10 sts.

Round 2 (inc): 3ch (counts as 1tr), 1 tr into same st, (2tr in next st) 9 times, ss into top of 3 ch. 20 sts.

Round 3 (inc): 4ch (counts as 1tr, 1ch), (1tr in next st, 1ch) 19 times, ss into 3rd of 4 ch at beg of round. 40 sts.

Round 4 (inc): Ss into next ch sp, 4ch (counts as 1tr, 1ch), (tr5tog into next ch sp, 1ch, 1tr into next ch sp, 1ch) 9 times, tr5tog in next ch sp, 1ch, ss into 3rd of 4 ch at beg of round.

Round 5 (inc): 4ch (counts as 1tr, 1ch), *tr5tog into next ch sp, 1ch, tr5tog into next ch sp, 1 ch, 1 tr into top of next tr, 1ch; rep from * 8 times more, tr5tog in next ch sp, 1ch, tr5tog in next ch sp, 1ch, ss into 3rd of 4 ch at beg of round.

Round 6 (inc): 4ch (counts as 1tr, 1ch), *(tr5tog into next ch sp, 1ch) 3 times, 1 tr into top of next tr, 1 ch; rep from * 8 times more, (tr5tog in next ch sp, 1ch) 3 times, ss into 3rd of 4ch at beg of round.

Round 7 (inc): 4ch (counts as 1tr, 1ch), 1 tr into next ch sp, 1ch, *(tr5tog in next ch sp, 1ch) twice, 1tr in next ch sp, 1ch, 1tr into top of next tr, 1ch, 1 tr in next ch sp, 1ch; rep from * 8 times more, 1 tr in next ch sp, 1ch, ss into 3rd of 4th ch at beg of round.

Round 8 (inc): 4ch (counts as 1tr, 1ch), 1tr into top of next tr, 1ch, 1tr in next ch sp, 1ch, *tr5tog in next ch sp, 1ch, 1tr in next ch sp, 1ch, (1tr into top of next tr, 1ch) 3 times, 1tr in next ch sp, 1ch; rep from * 8 times more, tr5tog in next ch sp, 1ch, 1tr in next ch sp, 1ch, 1tr into top of next tr, 1ch, ss into 3rd of 4th ch at beg of round.

Round 9 (inc): 4ch (counts as 1tr, 1ch), (1tr into top of next tr, 1ch) twice, *(1tr in next ch sp, 1ch) twice, (1tr into top of next tr, 1 ch) 5 times; rep from * 8 more times, (1tr in next ch sp, 1ch) twice, (1tr into top of next tr, 1ch)

twice, ss into 3rd of 4th ch at beg of round. 140 sts.

Round 10: 4ch (counts as 1tr, 1ch), (1tr into top of next tr, 1ch) 69 times, ss into 3rd of 4th ch at beg of round.

Round 11 & 12: Work as round 10.

Round 13 (dec): 4ch (counts as 1tr, 1ch) 1tr into top of next tr, 1ch, *(tr2tog, 1ch) twice, (1tr into top of next tr, 1ch) three times; rep from * 8 times more, (tr2tog, 1ch) twice, 1tr into top of next tr, 1ch, ss into 3rd of 4th ch at beg of round. 100 sts.

Round 14 (dec): 4ch (counts as 1tr, 1ch), *(tr2tog into next 2 tr, 1ch, tr5tog into next ch sp, 1ch, tr2tog into next 2 tr, 1ch, 1tr into top of next tr, 1ch; rep from * 8 times more, tr2tog into next 2 tr, 1ch, tr5tog into next ch sp, 1ch, tr2tog into next 2 tr, 1ch, ss into 3rd of 4th ch at beg of round.

Round 15: 4ch (counts as 1tr, 1ch), 1tr into top of next tr, 1ch, *(tr5tog into next ch sp, 1ch) twice, (1tr into top of next tr, 1ch) three times; rep from * 8 times more, (tr5tog into next ch sp, 1ch) twice, 1tr into top of next tr, 1ch, ss into 3rd of 4th ch at beg of round.

Round 16: 2ch (counts as 1htr), 1htr in next ch sp, *1htr into top of next tr, miss next ch sp, 1htr into top of cluster, 1htr into ch sp, 1htr into top of cluster, miss next ch sp, (1htr into top of next tr, 1htr into next ch sp) twice; rep from * 8 times more, 1htr into top of next tr, miss next ch sp, 1htr into top of cluster, 1htr into ch sp, 1htr into top of cluster, miss next ch sp, 1htr into top of next tr, 1htr into next ch sp, ss into 2nd of 2 ch at beg of round. 80 sts.

Round 17: 2ch (counts as 1htr), (1htr into next st) 79 times, ss into 1st st.
Change to 3.25 mm (US D3) hook.

Round 18: 1ch (counts as 1 dc), (1dc into next st) 79 times, ss into 1st st.

Rounds 19, 20 , 21 & 22: As round 18.
Finishing round: Work 1dc back into last st worked on previous round, *1dc into next stitch to right; rep from * to end.
Fasten off.

BUTTERCUP
LACY SHRUG WITH FRONT TIES

Recommendation
Suitable for the knitter with a little experience.
Please see pages 28 & 29 for photographs.

	XS	S	M	L	XL	XXL	
To fit	**81**	**86**	**91**	**97**	**102**	**109**	**cm**
bust	32	34	36	38	40	43	in

Rowan Milk Cotton Fine

5	5	6	6	6	7	x 50gm

Photographed in Liquorice

Button – 4 small

Needles
1 pair 2¼ mm (no 13) (US 1) needles
1 pair 2¾ mm (no 12) (US 2) needles

Tension
21 sts and 42 rows to 10 cm measured over
pattern using 2¾ mm (US 2) needles.

Special abbreviations
MP = make picot: cast on 1 st, cast off 1 st.
Inc 2 = inc 2 sts by knitting into front, back
and front again of next st.

Note: As the number of working sts varies
greatly within this lace pattern, it is important
to remember that the number of sts quoted
within the pattern refer to the 'real' number of
sts and not the number of sts on the needles
after working rows 3 and 10 of the patt repeat.
Please bear this in mind when checking your
work. To make the shapings easier to work
within the patt repeat, we have used double
incs and decs, thus allowing the inc sts to be
easily accommodated into the patt repeat.

BACK
Cast on 74 (80: 86: 90: 96) sts using
2¾ mm (US 2) needles and work in
patt as folls:
Row 1 (RS): Knit.
Row 2: Knit.
Row 3: K1 (2: 1: 1: 2), *yo, K1, rep from * to
last 1 (2: 1: 1: 2) sts, K1 (2: 1: 1: 2).
Row 4: Purl.
Row 5: K1 (2: 1: 1: 2), *K2tog, rep from *
to last 1 (2:1: 1: 2) sts, K1 (2: 1: 1: 2).
Rows 6 & 7: K1 (2: 1: 1: 2), *yo, K2tog,
rep from * to last 1 (2: 1: 1: 2) sts, K1
(2: 1: 1: 2).
Rows 8 (WS): Knit.
Row 9: Knit.
Row 10: Work as row 3.
Row 11: Work as row 4.
Row 12: Work as row 5.
Rows 13 & 14: Work as rows 6 and 7.
These 14 rows form the patt and are repeated
throughout.
Cont in patt for a further 8 rows, ending with
a WS row.
Next row (RS) (inc): Inc 2, patt to last st, inc
2. 78 (84: 90: 94: 100) sts.
Work 27 rows in patt.
Inc as before on next row.
82 (88: 94: 98: 104) sts.
Work 17 (21: 25: 27: 29) rows, ending with
a WS row.
Shape armholes
Keeping patt correct, cast off 4 sts at beg
of next 2 rows.
74 (80: 86: 90: 96) sts.
Next row (RS) (dec): K3tog, patt to last 3 sts,
K3tog.
Work 1 row.
Dec as before on next row and foll 0 (1: 1: 1:
1) alt rows.
Work 5 (5: 5: 5: 3) rows.
Dec as before on next row and then for **largest
size only** on foll 6th row.
62 (64: 70: 74: 76) sts.
Cont straight until armhole measures 17 (17:
18: 19: 19) cm.

Shape shoulders and back neck
Making sure any extra patt sts are taken into
consideration, cast off 7 (6: 8: 8: 8) sts, patt
until there are 14 (14: 15: 15: 16) sts on right
needle and turn, leaving rem sts on a holder.
Work each side of neck separately.
Dec 1 st at at beg of next row.
Cast off 6 (6: 7: 7: 7) sts at beg and dec 1 st
at end of next row.
Work 1 row.
Cast off rem 6 (6: 6: 6: 7) sts.
With RS facing, rejoin yarn to rem sts, cast off
centre 20 (24: 24: 28: 28) sts, patt to end.
Complete to match first side, reversing
shapings.

LEFT FRONT
Cast on 43 (46: 49: 51: 54) sts using 2¾ mm
(US 2) needles, and work in patt as folls:.
Row 1 (RS): Knit.
Row 2: MP, K to end.
Row 3: K1 (2: 1: 1: 2), *yo, K1, rep from * to
last 12 sts, K12.
Row 4: MP, K until 12 st on right needle, P to
end.
Row 5: K1 (2: 1: 1: 2), *K2tog, rep from * to
last 12 sts, K12.
Row 6: MP, K until 12 on right needle, *yo,
K2tog, rep from * to last 1 (2: 1: 1: 2) sts,
K1 (2: 1: 1: 2).
Row 7: K1 (2: 1: 1: 2), *yo, K2tog, rep from *
to last 12 sts, K12.
Row 8 (WS): MP, K to end.
Row 9: Knit.
Row 10: MP, K until 12 sts on right needle,
*yo, K1, rep from * to last 1 (2: 1: 1: 2) sts,
K1 (2: 1: 1: 2).
Row 11: P to last 12 sts, K12.
Row 12: MP, K until 12 on right needle,
*K2tog, rep from * to last 1 (2: 1: 1: 2) sts, K1
(2: 1: 1: 2).
Row 13: K1 (2: 1: 1: 2), *yo, K2tog, rep from *
to last 12 sts, K12.
Row 14: MP, K until 12 sts on right needle,
*yo, K2tog, rep from * to last 1 (2: 1: 1: 2) sts,
K1 (2: 1: 1: 2).

These 14 rows form the patt and are repeated throughout.

Cont in patt for a further 8 rows, ending with a WS row.

Shape side and front edge

Next row (inc) (dec): Inc 2, patt to last 15 sts, K3tog tbl, K12.

Work 27 rows.

1st, 2nd and 3rd sizes only:

Next row (inc): Inc 2, patt to end.

45 (48: 51) sts.

Work 11 (5: 5) rows.

Next row (dec): Patt to last 15 sts, K3tog tbl, K12.

Work 5 (15: 19) rows, ending with a WS row.

Shape armhole

Cast off 4 sts at beg of next row.

39 (42: 45) sts.

Work 1 row, ending with a WS row.

4th and 5th sizes only:

Next row (inc) (dec): Inc 2, patt to last 15 sts, K3tog tbl, K12.

Work 27 (29) rows, ending with a WS row.

Shape armhole

Next row (dec): Cast off 4 sts at beg of next row, patt to last 15 sts, K3tog tbl, K12.

45 (48) sts.

Work 1 row, ending with a WS row.

All sizes:

Next row (RS) (dec): K3 tog, patt to end

Work 1 row.

Dec as before on next row and 0 (1: 1: 1: 1) foll alt row.

Work 5 (5: 5: 5: 3) rows.

Dec as before on next row, and then for **largest size only** on foll 6th row.

33 (34: 37: 37: 38) sts.

Work 23 (5: 1: 17: 11) rows, ending with a WS row.

Dec 2 sts as before at neck edge on next row, and then for **2nd, 3rd, 4th and 5th size only** foll – (34th: 34th: 28th: 28th) row.

31 (30: 33: 33: 34) sts.

Cont until left front matches back to start of shoulder shaping, ending with a WS row.

Shape shoulder

Cast off 7 (6: 8: 8: 8) sts at beg of next row and 6 (6: 7: 7: 7) sts at beg of foll alt row.

Work 1 row.

Cast off 6 (6: 6: 6: 7), K to end. 12 sts.

Cont on these 12 sts for a further 6.5 (7: 7: 7.5: 7.5) cm (when slightly stretched).

Cast off.

RIGHT FRONT

Cast on 43 (46: 49: 51: 54) sts using 2¾ mm (US 2) needles, and work in patt as folls:

Row 1 (RS): MP, K to end.

Row 2: Knit.

Row 3: MP, K until 12 sts on right needle, *yo, K1, rep from * to last 1 (2: 1: 1: 2) sts, K1 (2: 1: 1: 2).

Row 4: Purl to last 12 sts, K12.

Row 5: MP, K until 12 sts on right needle, *K2tog, rep from * to last 1 (2: 1: 1: 2) sts, K1 (2: 1: 1: 2).

Row 6: K1 (2: 1: 1: 2), *yo, K2tog, rep from * to last 12 sts, K12.

Row 7: MP, K until 12 sts on right needle, *yo, K2tog, rep from * to last 1 (2: 1: 1: 2) st, K1 (2: 1: 1: 2).

Row 8 (WS): Knit.

Row 9: MP, K to end.

Row 10: K1 (2: 1: 1: 2), *yo, K1, rep from * to last 12 sts, K12.

Row 11: MP, K until 12 sts on right needle, P to end.

Row 12: K1 (2: 1: 1: 2), *K2tog, rep from * to last 12sts, K12.

Row 13: MP, K until 12 sts on right needle, *yo, K2tog, rep from * to last 1 (2:1: 1: 2) sts, K1 (2: 1: 1: 2).

Row 14: K1 (2: 1: 1: 2), *yo, K2tog, rep from * to last 12 sts, K12.

These 14 rows form the patt and are repeated throughout.

Cont in patt for a further 8 rows, ending with a WS row.

Shape side and front edge

Next row (inc) (dec): MP, K until 12 sts on right needle, K3tog, patt to last st, inc 2.

Work 27 rows.

Complete as for left front, reversing shapings.

SLEEVES (both alike)

(N.B. Sleeve has a vent half way across sleeve.)

First side

**Using 2¼ mm (US 1) needles, work picot cast-on as folls:

Cast on 4 sts, cast off 1 st, slip loop on right needle back to left needle, *cast on 3 sts, cast off 1 st, slip loop on right needle back to left needle, rep from * until there are 29 (29: 31: 31: 33) sts on needle, cast on 0 (1: 0: 1: 0) st. 29 (30: 31: 32: 33) sts. **

Row 1 (RS): MP, K to end.

Row 2: Knit.

Rep these 2 rows 4 times more, inc 1 st at beg of rows 6 and 10.

31 (32: 33: 34: 35) sts.

Change to 2¾ mm (US 2) and cont in patt as folls:

Row 1 (RS): MP, K until 2 sts on right needle, *yo, K1, rep from * to last 1 (2: 1: 2: 1) sts, K1 (2: 1: 2: 1).

Row 2: Purl to last 2 sts, K2.

Row 3: MP, K until 2 sts on right needle, *K2tog, rep from * to last 1(2: 1: 2: 1) sts, K1 (2: 1: 2: 1).

Row 4: K1 (2: 1: 2: 1), *yo, K2tog, rep from * to last 2 sts, K2.

Row 5: MP, K until 2 sts on right needle, *yo, K2tog, rep from * to last 1 (2: 1: 2: 1) sts, K1 (2:1: 2: 1).

Row 6 (WS): Knit.

These 6 rows set the sts for the 14 row patt rep as on back.

Keeping patt correct, work 3 (5: 7: 9: 11) rows, ending with a **RS** row.

Shape top

Taking extra patt sts into consideration, cast off 4 sts at beg of next row.

Next row (dec): Patt to last 3 sts, K3 tog.

Work 3 rows, ending with a WS row.

Break yarn and leave sts on a spare needle.

Second side

Work as given for first side from ** to **.

Row 1 (RS): Knit.

Row 2: MP, K to end.

Rep these 2 rows 4 times more, inc 1 st at end of rows 6 and 10.

31 (32: 33: 34: 35) sts.

Change to 2¾ mm (US 2) and cont in patt as folls:

Row 1: K1 (2: 1: 2: 1), *yo, K1, rep from * to last 2 sts, K2.

Row 2: M1,K1, P to end.

Row 3: K1 (2: 1: 2: 1), *K2tog, rep from * to last 2 sts, K2.

Row 4: M1,K1, *yo, K2tog, rep from * to last 1 (2: 1: 2: 1) sts, K1 (2: 1: 2: 1).

Row 5: K1 (2: 1: 2: 1), *yo, K2tog, rep from * to last 2 sts, K2.

Row 6 (WS): MP, K to end.

These 6 rows set the sts for the 14 row patt rep as on back.

Keeping patt correct, work 2 (4: 6: 8: 10) rows, ending with a WS row.

Shape top

Cast off 4 sts at beg of next row.

Work 1 row.

Next row (dec): K3 tog, patt to end.

Work 3 rows, ending with a WS row.

Join sides together as folls:

Next row (RS): Patt across sts of second side as folls: K3tog, patt to end, patt across sts of first side to last 3 sts, K3tog.

46 (48: 50: 52: 54) sts.

Work 5 rows in patt.

Dec 2 st at each end of next row, then on foll 8th row, then on 1 (1: 1: 2: 2) foll 10th rows.

34 (36: 38: 36: 38) sts.

Work 7 rows.

Dec 2 sts at each end of next row, then on 0 (1: 1: 0: 0) foll 6th row, then on 2 foll alt rows.

22 (20: 22: 24: 26) sts.

Work 1 row.

1st size only

Dec 2 sts at each end of next row. 18 sts.

All sizes

Cast off.

MAKING UP

Press all pieces using a warm iron over a damp cloth.

Join shoulder seams using back stitch or mattress stitch if preferred.

Join the cast-off edges of the extended front edgings neatly together, and slip stitch in place around back neck.

Join side and sleeve seams.

Set sleeves into armholes.

Tie

Using 2¼ mm (US 1) needles, work picot caston as folls:

Cast on 4 sts, cast off 1 st, slip loop on right needle back to left needle, *cast on 3 sts, cast off 1 st, slip loop on right needle back to left needle, rep from * until there are 15 (15: 15: 17: 17) sts on needle.

Row 1 (RS): MP, K to last 2 sts, inc in next st, K1. 16 (16: 16: 18: 18) sts.

Row 2: MP, K to last 2 sts, K2tog tbl. 15 (15: 15: 17: 17) sts.

Rep these 2 rows until belt measure 135 (140: 145: 150: 155) cm.

Picot cast off: Cast off 2 sts, *slip st on right needle onto left needle, cast on 2 sts, cast off 4 sts, rep from * to end.

Sew the tie into place around the lower edge, overlapping the tie onto the garment.

Stitch neatly into place.

Button loops for sleeves (both alike)

Make 2 short chains and sew into place on row-ends of the garter stitch on the sleeve front. Sew buttons into place on the sleeve back to correspond with loops.

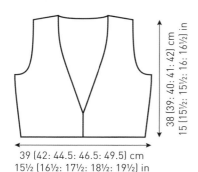

39 (42: 44.5: 46.5: 49.5) cm
15½ (16½: 17½: 18½: 19½) in

38 (39: 40: 41: 42) cm
15 (15½: 15½: 16: 16½) in

4 (4: 5: 5: 6) cm
1½ (1½: 2: 2: 2½) in

Recommendation

Suitable for the knitter with a little experience.
Please see pages 32 & 33 for photographs.

	XS	S	M	L	XL	XXL	
To fit	**81**	**86**	**91**	**97**	**102**	**107**	**cm**
bust	32	34	36	38	40	42	in

Rowan Wool Cotton

10 11 12 12 13 13 x 50gm
Photographed in Misty

Buttons – 3

Needles

1 pair 2¾ mm (no 12) (US 2) needles
1 pair 3 mm (no 11)(US 2/3) needles
1 pair 3¼ mm (no 10) (US 3) needles

Tension

26 sts and 36 rows to 10 cm measured over
textured pattern using 3¼ mm (US 3)
needles.

Special abbreviation:

MP = Make picot: cast on 1 st, cast off 1 st.
(See information page for details)

ALI
SHAWL COLLARED BASKET WEAVE STITCH JACKET

BACK

Cast on 105 (111: 119: 125: 133: 141) sts
using 3 mm (US 2/3) needles and work 20
rows in garter st, ending with a WS row.
Mark the 25th (26th: 27th: 28th: 29th: 30th)
st in from each end of last row.
Next row (RS)(dec): K2, K2tog, (K to 3 sts
before marker, K2tog, K3, K2tog tbl) twice,
K to last 4 sts, K2tog tbl, K2.
99 (105: 113: 119: 127: 135) sts.
Work 19 rows, ending with a WS row.
Dec as before on next row and foll 20th row.
87 (93: 101: 107: 115: 123) sts.
Work 7 (9: 9: 11: 11: 13) rows, ending with
a WS row.
Change to 3¼ mm (US 3) needles and cont
in textured patt as folls:
Row 1 (RS): Knit.
Row 2: P0 (1: 0: 0: 0: 4), K5 (7: 0: 3: 7: 7),
*P5, K7, rep from * to last 10 (1: 5: 8: 0: 4)
sts, P5 (1: 5: 5: 0: 4), K5 (0: 0: 3: 0: 0).
Row 3: K0 (1: 0: 0: 0: 4), P5 (7: 0: 3: 7: 7),
*K5, P7, rep from * to last 10 (1: 5: 8: 0: 4)
sts, K5 (1: 5: 5: 0: 4), P5 (0: 0: 3: 0: 0).
Rows 4 and 5: As rows 2 and 3.
Row 6: As row 2.
Row 7: Knit.
Row 8: P4 (0: 0: 2: 0: 0), K7 (2: 6: 7: 1:
5), *P5, K7, rep from * to last 4 (7: 11: 2:
6: 10) sts, P4 (5: 5: 2: 5: 5), K0 (2: 6: 0:
1: 5).
Row 9: Inc in first st, K3 (0: 0: 1: 0: 0), P7
(1: 5: 7: 0: 4), *K5, P7, rep from * to last 4
(7: 11: 2: 6: 10) sts, K3 (5: 5: 1: 5: 5), P0
(1: 5: 0: 0: 4), inc in last st.
Row 10: P0 (0: 0: 3: 0: 0), K0 (3: 7: 7: 2:
6), *P5, K7, rep from * to last 5 (8: 0: 3:
7: 11) sts, P5 (5: 0: 3: 5: 5), K0 (3: 0: 0:
2: 6).
Row 11: K0 (0: 0: 3: 0: 0), P0 (3: 7: 7: 2:
6), *K5, P7, rep from * to last 5 (8: 0: 3:
7: 11) sts, K5 (5: 0: 3: 5: 5), P0 (3: 0: 0:
2: 6).
Row 12: As row 10.
These 12 rows form textured patt and start
side seam shaping.

Cont in patt, inc 1 st at each end of 4 foll 8th
rows, then on every foll 6th row until there are
105 (111: 119: 125: 133: 141) sts, taking inc
sts into patt.
Cont straight until back measures 35 (35: 36:
36: 37: 37) cm, ending with a WS row.
Shape armholes
Keeping patt correct, cast off 3 (3: 5: 5: 6: 6)
sts at beg of next 2 rows.
99 (105: 109: 115: 121: 129) sts.
Dec 1 st at each end of next 5 (5: 5: 7: 7: 9)
rows, then on every foll alt row until 81 (85:
89: 91: 95: 99) sts rem.
Cont straight until armhole measures 18 (19:
19: 20: 20: 21) cm, ending with a WS row.
Shape shoulders and back neck
Cast off 7 (8: 8: 8: 9: 9) sts at beg of next
2 rows.
67 (69: 73: 75: 77: 81) sts.
Cast off 7 (8: 8: 8: 9: 9) sts at beg of next
row, patt until there are 12 (11: 13: 13: 13:
14) sts on RH needle and turn, leaving rem
sts on a holder.
Work each side of neck separately.
Cast off 4 sts at beg of next row.
Cast off rem 8 (7: 9: 9: 9: 10) sts.
With RS facing, rejoin yarn to sts from holder,
cast off centre 29 (31: 31: 33: 33: 35) sts,
patt to end.
Work to match first side, reversing shaping.

LEFT FRONT

Cast on 62 (65: 69: 72: 76: 80) sts using
3 mm (US 2/3) needles and cont in garter
st with picot edging as folls:
Row 1 (RS): Knit.
Row 2: MP, K to end.
Rows 3 and 4: Knit.
These 4 rows form garter st with picot
edging. Working a picot on every foll 4th row
throughout, cont as folls:
Work a further 16 rows as set, ending with
a WS row.
Mark the 25th (26th: 27th: 28th: 29th:
30th) st in from end (side seam edge)
of last row.

Next row (RS)(dec): K2, K2tog, K to 3 sts before marker, K2tog, K3, K2tog tbl, K to end.
59 (62: 66: 69: 73: 77) sts.
Work 19 rows, ending with a WS row.
Dec as before on next row and foll 20th row.
53 (56: 60: 63: 67: 71) sts.
Work 7 (9: 9: 11: 11: 13) rows, ending with a WS row.
Change to 3¼ mm (US 3) needles and cont in textured patt as folls:
Row 1 (RS): Knit.
Row 2: (MP) 1 (0: 0: 1: 1: 0) times, K until there are 19 sts on RH needle, *P5, K7, rep from * to last 10 (1: 5: 8: 0: 4) sts, P5 (1: 5: 5: 0: 4), K5 (0: 0: 3: 0: 0).
Row 3: K0 (1: 0: 0: 0: 4), P5 (7: 0: 3: 7: 7), *K5, P7, rep from * to last 19 sts, P6, K to end.
Row 4: (MP) 0 (1: 1: 0: 0: 1) times, K until there are 19 sts on RH needle, *P5, K7, rep from * to last 10 (1: 5: 8: 0: 4) sts, P5 (1: 5: 5: 0: 4), K5 (0: 0: 3: 0: 0).
Row 5: As row and 3.
Row 6: As row 2.
Row 7: Knit.
Row 8: (MP) 0 (1: 1: 0: 0: 1) times, K until there are 13 sts on RH needle, *P5, K7, rep from * to last 4 (7: 11: 2: 6: 10) sts, P4 (5: 5: 2: 5: 5), K0 (2: 6: 0: 1: 5).
Row 9: Inc in first st, K3 (0: 0: 1: 0: 0), P7 (1: 5: 7: 0: 4), *K5, P7, rep from * to last 18 sts, K to end.
Row 10: (MP) 1 (0: 0: 1: 1: 0) times, K until there are 13 sts on RH needle, *P5, K7, rep from * to last 5 (8: 0: 3: 7: 11) sts, P5 (5: 0: 3: 5: 5), K0 (3: 0: 0: 2: 6).
Row 11: K0 (0: 0: 3: 0: 0), P0 (3: 7: 7: 2: 6), *K5, P7, rep from * to last 18 sts, K to end.
Row 12: (MP) 0 (1: 1: 0: 0: 1) times, K until there are 13 sts on RH needle, *P5, K7, rep from * to last 5 (8: 0: 3: 7: 11) sts, P5 (5: 0: 3: 5: 5), K0 (3: 0: 0: 2: 6).
These 12 rows form textured patt and start side seam shaping.
Cont in patt, inc 1 st at beg of 4 foll 8th rows, then on foll 6th row, taking inc sts into patt.
59 (62: 66: 69: 73: 77) sts.
Shape collar
Next row (RS)(inc): Inc in first st, patt to last 13 sts, M1, K to end.
Next row: (MP) 0 (1: 1: 0: 0: 1) times, K until there are 15 sts on RH needle, patt to end.
Work 2 rows.
Next row: Inc in first st, patt to end.

Next row: (MP) 0 (1: 1: 0: 0: 1) times, K until there are 16 sts on RH needle, patt to end.
Work 2 rows.
Next row: Patt to last 16 sts, M1, K to end.
Next row: (MP) 0 (1: 1: 0: 0: 1) times, K until there are 18 sts on RH needle, patt to end.
Next row: Inc in first st, patt to end.
Next row: (MP) 1 (0: 0: 1: 1: 0) times, K until there are 18 sts on RH needle, patt to end.
Work 1 row.
Next row (WS): (MP) 0 (1: 1: 0: 0: 1) times, K until there are 19 sts on RH needle, patt to end.
Work 2 rows.
Next row: Patt to last 19 sts, M1, K to end.
Next row: (MP) 0 (1: 1: 0: 0: 1) times, K until there are 21 sts on RH needle, patt to end.
Taking 1 extra st into garter st on every foll 4th row until there are 32 (33: 33: 34: 34: 35) sts in garter st, cont without any further side seam shaping until left front matches back to beg of armhole shaping, ending with a WS row.
65 (68: 72: 75: 79: 83) sts.
Shape armhole
Keeping patt correct, cast off 3 (3: 5: 5: 6: 6) sts at beg of next row.
62 (65: 67: 70: 73: 77) sts.
Work 1 row.
Next row: Work 2tog, patt to garter st collar, M1, K to end.
Cont in patt, inc 1 st at inside edge of collar shaping as before on 0 (0: 1: 1: 2: 2) foll 8th rows, and **at the same time,** shape armhole as folls:
Dec 1 st at armhole edge of next 4 (4: 4: 6: 6: 8) rows, then on every foll alt row until 54 (56: 59: 60: 63: 65) sts rem.
Cont in patt as set until left front matches back to start of shoulder shaping, ending with a WS row.
Shape shoulder
Cast off 7 (8: 8: 8: 9: 9) sts at beg of next and foll alt row.
Work 1 row.
Next row (RS): Cast off 8 (7: 9: 9: 9: 10) sts, patt to end. 32 (33: 34: 35: 36: 37) sts.
Work a further 26 (28: 28: 32: 32: 36) rows on these 32 (33: 34: 35: 36: 37) sts, ending with a **RS** row.
Next row (WS of garment, RS of collar): Patt 27 (28: 29: 30: 31: 32) sts, wrap next st, turn and K to end.

Next row: Patt 19 (20: 22: 22: 23: 24) sts, wrap next st, turn and K to end.
Next row: Patt 11 (12: 13: 14: 15: 16) sts, wrap next st, turn and K to end.
Knit 1 row.
Cast off.
Mark the positions of 3 buttonholes on left front, the second one to come at top of garter st, the first and last ones to come 18 rows either side of the second one.

RIGHT FRONT
Cast on 62 (65: 69: 72: 76: 80) sts using 3 mm (US 2/3) needles and cont in garter st with picot edging as folls:
Row 1 (RS): MP, K to end.
Rows 2–4: Knit.
These 4 rows form garter st with picot edging. Working a picot on every foll 4th row throughout, cont as folls:
Work a further 16 rows as set, ending with a WS row.
Mark the 25th (26th: 27th: 28th: 29th: 30th) st in from beg (side seam edge) of last row.
Next row (RS)(dec): K2, K2tog, K to 3 sts before marker, K2tog, K3, K2tog tbl, K to end.
59 (62: 66: 69: 73: 77) sts.
Work 19 rows, ending with a WS row.
Dec as before on next row.
Work 9 (11: 11: 13: 13: 15) rows, ending with a WS row.
Next row (RS)(buttonhole row): Patt 6, cast off 3 sts, patt to end and back, casting on 3 sts over those cast off on previous row.
Working 2 further buttonholes in this way to correspond with positions marked for buttons, cont as folls:
Work 8 (6: 6: 4: 4: 2) rows, ending with a WS row.
Dec as before on next row.
53 (56: 60: 63: 67: 71) sts.
Work 7 (9: 9: 11: 11: 13) rows, ending with a WS row.
Change to 3¼ mm (US 3) needles and cont in textured patt as folls:
Row 1 (RS): (MP) 1 (0: 0: 1: 1: 0) times, K to end.
Row 2: P0 (1: 0: 0: 0: 4), K5 (7: 0: 3: 7: 7), *P5, K7, rep from * to last 12 sts, K to end.
Row 3: (MP) 0 (1: 1: 0: 0: 1) times, patt until there are 13 sts on RH needle, P6, *K5, P7, rep from * to last 10 (1: 5: 8: 0: 4) sts, K5 (1: 5: 5: 0: 4), P5 (0: 0: 3: 0: 0).

These 2 rows set the position of patt as on back.
Keeping patt correct, complete to match left front, reversing all shapings.

SLEEVES (both alike)

Cast on 63 (65: 67: 69: 71: 73) sts using 3 mm (US 2/3) needles and work 20 rows in garter st, inc 1 st at each end of 15th of these row, and ending with a WS row.
65 (67: 69: 71: 73: 75) sts.
Change to 3¼ mm (US 3) needles and cont in textured patt as folls:
Row 1 (RS): Knit.
Row 2: P0 (0: 1: 2: 3: 4), K6 (7: 7: 7: 7: 7), *P5, K7, rep from * to last 11 (0: 1: 2: 3: 4) sts, P5 (0: 1: 2: 3: 4), K6 (0: 0: 0: 0: 0).
This row sets position of textured patt as given for back.
Keeping patt correct, inc 1 st at each end of next row, then on every foll 12th row to 77 (81: 77: 81: 77: 81) sts, then on every foll 10th (-: 10th: 10th: 10th: 10th:) row until there are 79 (-: 85: 87: 91: 93) sts, taking inc sts into patt.
Cont straight until sleeve measures 32 (33: 34: 35: 36: 37) cm, ending with a WS row.
Shape sleevehead
Keeping patt correct, cast off 3 (3: 5: 5: 6: 6) sts at beg of next 2 rows.
73 (75: 75: 77: 79: 81) sts.
Dec 1 st at each end of next 3 rows, then on 2 foll alt rows.
Work 3 rows, ending with a WS row.
Dec 1 st at each end of next row and every foll 4th row until 49 (49: 49: 49: 51: 51) sts rem.
Work 1 row.
Dec 1 st at each end of next row and 2 foll alt rows, then on every foll row until 37 (37: 37: 37: 39: 39) sts rem, ending with a WS row.
Cast off.

MAKING UP

Press as described on information page.
Join both shoulder seams using backstitch or mattress stitch if preferred.
With RS facing, join shaped ends collar, then stitch neatly in place around back neck.
Join side and sleeve seams.
Set sleeves in to armholes using the set-in method.
Sew on buttons to correspond with buttonholes.

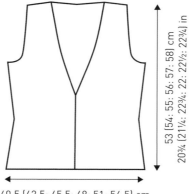

53 [54: 55: 56: 57: 58] cm
20¾ [21¼: 21¾: 22: 22½: 22¾] in

40.5 (42.5: 45.5: 48: 51: 54.5) cm
16 (16¾: 18: 19: 20: 21½) in

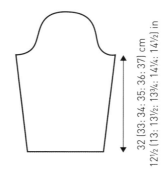

32 [33: 34: 35: 36: 37] cm
12½ [13: 13½: 13¾: 14¼: 14½] in

BLITHE
BUTTON THROUGH CAPPED SLEEVE VEST

Recommendation
Suitable for the knitter with a little experience.
Please see pages 22 & 23 for photographs.

	XS	S	M	L	XL	XXL	
To fit	**81**	**86**	**91**	**97**	**102**	**109**	**cm**
bust	32	34	36	38	40	43	in

Rowan Milk Cotton Fine

	5	5	6	6	6	7	x 50gm

Photographed in Pastille

Buttons – 7

Needles
1 pair 2 ¼ mm (no 13) (US 1) needles
1 pair 2 ¾ mm (no 12) (US 2) needles

Tension
29 sts and 38 rows to 10 cm measured over
stocking stitch using 2 ¾ mm (US 2) needles.

Pattern note: When knitting fronts, it is
advisable to join in new balls of yarn at side
seam or armhole edge so that front opening
edge remains neat and tidy as there are no
front opening edgings added afterwards.

Horizontal rib pattern:
Row 1 (RS): Purl.
Rows 2 & 3: Knit.
Row 4: Purl.
These 4 rows form the pattern.

Ridge pattern:
Rows 1, 3 & 5: Knit.
Rows 2, 4 & 6: Purl.
Row 7 (RS): Purl.
Row 8: Knit.
These 8 rows form the pattern.

FRONT
Cast on 117 (123: 131: 137: 147: 157) sts
using 2 ¼ mm (US 1) needles and work lower
edging as folls:
Purl 4 rows.
Starting with patt row 1, work 18 rows in
horizontal rib patt as given above, ending with
a WS row. **
Change to 2 ¾ mm (US 2) needles and
cont shaping sides and setting sts for
the centre panel worked in **ridge pattern**
as folls:
Row 1 (dec) (RS): K2, K2tog, K to last 4 sts,
K2tog tbl, K2.
115 (121: 129: 135: 145: 155) sts.
Rows 2, 4 & 6: Purl.
Rows 3 & 5: Knit.
Row 7 (RS): K26 (28: 31: 32: 36: 39), P63
(65: 67: 71: 73: 77) (for centre panel), K26
(28: 31: 32: 36: 39).
Row 8: P26 (28: 31: 32: 36: 39), K63 (65:
67: 71: 73: 77), P26 (28: 31: 32: 36: 39).
The last 8 rows form the patt and set the
sts for the front panel, and are repeated
throughout.
Cont in patt, working centre panel as set,
and **at same time** dec 1 st at each end
of next and 3 foll 8th rows, ending with
a **RS** row.
107 (113: 121: 127: 137: 147) sts.
Keeping patt correct, work 23 rows
straight, ending after patt row 8 and
with a WS row.

Divide for front opening
Next row (RS): Patt 50 (53: 57: 60: 64: 69)
sts and slip these onto a holder for left front,
patt to end.
57 (60: 64: 67: 73: 78) sts.
Work each side of front separately.
Work 1 row.
Cont in patt but now work the 7 (7: 7: 7:
9: 9) sts at centre front in **horizontal rib**
patt to form buttonhole band, and place the
buttonholes as folls:
Row 1 (RS): P7 (7: 7: 7: 9: 9) (for front band),
K to end.
Row 2: P to last 7 (7: 7: 7: 9: 9) sts, K to end.
Row 3: Knit.
Row 4: Purl.
Row 5: P35 (36: 37: 39: 41: 43), K to end.
Row 6: P to last 35 (36: 37: 39: 41: 43) sts,
K to end.
Row 7 (buttonhole row) (RS): K2 (2: 2: 2:
3: 3), K2tog, yfwd, K to end.
Row 8: Purl.
These 8 rows form the patt and set the
stitches for the **horizontal** and **ridge** patts.
Cont in patt as set, working 6 more
buttonholes as before on every alt 7th patt
row (i.e. every 16th row from last buttonhole)
and at same time shape sides and armhole
as folls:
Next row (inc) (RS): Patt to last 2 sts, M1, K2.
58 (61: 65: 68: 74: 79) sts.
Work 11 rows.
Inc 1 st as before on next and foll 12th row,
then on 3 foll 10th rows, ending with a **RS** row.
63 (66: 70: 73: 79: 84) sts.
Work 12 (12: 12: 12: 14: 14) rows straight,
ending with a **RS** row.
Shape armhole
Keeping patt and buttonholes correct, cont as
folls:
Cast off 5 (5: 5: 5: 6: 6) sts at beg of next
row. 58 (61: 65: 68: 73: 78) sts.
Dec 1 st at armhole edge on next 7 (7: 7: 7:
9: 11) rows, then on foll 4 (4: 6: 6: 6: 5) alt
rows, and then on foll 4th row.
46 (49: 51: 54: 57: 61) sts.

Cont in patt until the 7th buttonhole row has been completed, ending with a RS row.

Work 1 row.

Shape front neck

Next row (RS): K16 (16: 17: 17: 17: 17) and slip these sts onto a holder for neck edging, patt to end.

30 (33: 34: 37: 40: 44) sts.

Dec 1 st at neck edge on next 6 (6: 8: 8: 8: 8) rows, then on every foll alt row until 20 (22: 23: 25: 26: 29) sts rem.

Work 3 rows.

Dec 1 st at neck edge on next and foll 4th row, and then on foll 6th row.

17 (19: 20: 22: 23: 26) sts.

Work straight until armhole measures 17 (18: 19: 19: 20: 21) cm, ending with a **RS** row.

Shape shoulder

Cast off 6 (6: 7: 7: 8: 9) sts at beg of next and foll alt row.

Work 1 row.

Cast off rem 5 (7: 6: 8: 7: 8) sts.

With WS facing, rejoin yarn to 50 (53: 57: 60: 64: 69) sts left on holder for left front, cast on 7 (7: 7: 7: 9: 9) sts, patt to end.

57 (60: 64: 67: 73: 78) sts.

Complete to match first side, reversing all shapings and omitting buttonholes.

BACK

Work as given for front to **.

Change to 2 ¾ mm (US 2) needles and cont in st st throughout, shaping sides as folls:

Next row (dec) (RS): K2, K2tog, K to last 4 sts, K2tog tbl, K2.

115 (121: 129: 135: 145: 155) sts.

Work 7 rows.

Dec 1 st as before at each end of next row and 3 foll 8th rows.

107 (113: 121: 127: 137: 147) sts.

Work 33 rows straight, ending with a WS row.

Next row (inc) (RS): K2, M1, K to last 2 sts, M1, K2. 109 (115: 123: 129: 139: 149) sts.

Work 11 rows.

Inc 1 st as before at each end of next row, then on foll 12th row, and then on 3 foll 10th rows.

119 (125: 133: 139: 149: 159) sts.

Work 11 (11: 11: 11: 13: 13) rows straight, ending with a WS row.

Shape armholes

Cast off 5 (5: 5: 5: 6: 6) sts at beg of next 2 rows.

109 (115: 123: 129: 137: 147) sts.

Dec 1 st at each end of next 7 (7: 7: 7: 9: 11) rows, then on 4 (4: 6: 6: 6: 5) foll alt rows, and then on foll 4th row.

85 (91: 95: 101: 105: 113) sts.

Work straight until back matches front to shoulder shaping, ending with a WS row.

Shape shoulders and back neck

Cast off 6 (6: 7: 7: 8: 9) sts at beg of next 2 rows. 73 (79: 81: 87: 89: 95) sts.

Next row (RS): Cast off 6 (6: 7: 7: 8: 9) sts, K until there are 9 (11: 10: 12: 11: 12) sts on right needle and turn, leaving rem sts on a holder.

Work each side of neck separately.

Cast off 4 sts at beg of next row.

Cast off rem 5 (7: 6: 8: 7: 8) sts.

With RS facing, rejoin yarn to rem sts, cast off centre 43 (45: 47: 49: 51: 53) sts, K to end.

Complete to match first side, reversing shapings.

Cap sleeves (make 2)

Cast on 8 (8: 9: 9: 10: 10) sts using 2 ¾ mm (US 2) needles.

Beg with patt row 1, work in **horizontal rib** patt as folls:

Work 8 rows.

Inc 1 st at beg of next and foll 4th row.

10 (10: 11: 11: 12: 12) sts.

Work 1 row, ending with a WS row.

Keeping patt correct, inc 1 st at beg of next and every foll alt row until there are 19 (19: 21: 21: 23: 23) sts.

Work 3 rows.

Inc 1 st at beg of next row.

20 (20: 22: 22: 24: 24) sts.

Work 59 (67: 71: 71: 75: 83) rows straight, ending with a WS row.

Dec 1 st at beg of next row, then on foll 4th row and then on every foll alt row until 11 (11: 12: 12: 13: 13) sts rem.

Work 3 rows, ending with a WS row.

Dec 1 st at beg of next and 2 foll 4th rows, ending with a **RS** row. 8 (8: 9: 9: 10: 10) sts.

Work 7 rows.

Cast off.

MAKING UP

Press all pieces using a warm iron over a damp cloth.

Join both shoulder seams.

Neck edging

With RS of right front facing and using 2 ¼ mm (US 1) needles, slip 16 (16: 17: 17: 17: 17) sts from holder onto right needle, rejoin yarn and pick up and knit 41 (44: 48: 52: 56: 60) sts up right side of neck, 51 (53: 55: 57: 59: 61) sts from back, and 41 (44: 48: 52: 56: 60) sts down left side of neck, then knit across 16 (16: 17: 17: 17: 17) sts from holder on left front.

165 (173: 185: 195: 205: 215) sts.

Beg with a K row, work 6 rows in rev st st.

Cast off knitwise (on WS).

Join side and sleeve seams.

Set shaped edge of capped sleeve into armholes.

Press seams and sew on buttons.

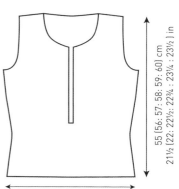

55 (56: 57: 58: 59: 60) cm
21½ (22: 22½: 22¾ : 23¼ : 23½) in

41 (43: 46: 48: 51.5: 55) cm
16¼ (17: 18: 19: 20¼ : 21¾) in

HUSH
SEMI FITTED DOUBLE MOSS STITCH CARDIGAN

Recommendation
Suitable for the knitter with a little experience.
Please see page 24 for photograph.

	XS	S	M	L	XL	XXL	
To fit	**81**	**86**	**91**	**97**	**102**	**109**	cm
bust	32	34	36	38	40	43	in

Rowan Denim
13	14	15	16	17	18x 50gm

Photographed in Ecru

Buttons – 7

Needles
1 pair 3 ¾ mm (no 9) (US 5) needles
1 pair 4 mm (no 8) (US 6) needles

Tension
Before washing: 22 sts and 30 rows to 10 cm
measured over double moss stitch using
4 mm (US 6) needles.

Tension note: Denim will shrink in length
when washed for the first time. Allowances
have been made in the pattern for shrinkage
(see size diagram for after washing
measurements).

Pattern note: When knitting fronts, it is
advisable to join in new balls of yarn at side
seam or armhole edge so that front opening
edge remains neat and tidy as there are no
front opening edgings added afterwards.

BACK
Cast on 89 (95: 101: 107: 113: 121) sts using
4 mm (US 6) needles and work in double
moss stitch, setting the stitches as folls:
Row 1 (RS): K0 (1: 0: 1: 0: 0), (P1, K1) to last
1 (0: 1: 0: 1: 1) sts, P1 (0: 1: 0: 1: 1).
Row 2: K1 (0: 1: 0: 1: 1), (P1, K1) to last
0 (1: 0: 1: 0: 0) sts, P0 (1: 0: 1: 0: 0).
Row 3: Work as row 2.
Row 4: Work as row 1.
These 4 rows form the patt and are rep throughout.
Work a further 8 (8: 10: 10: 10: 10) rows,
ending with a WS row.
Cont in patt, dec 1 st at each end of next row.
87 (93: 99: 105: 111: 119) sts.
Work 11 (11: 11: 13: 13: 13) rows.
Dec 1 st at each end of next row and foll
10th (10th: 12th: 12 th: 12th: 14th) row.
83 (89: 95: 101: 107: 115) sts.
Work 29 rows straight.
Inc 1 st at each end of next row and 2 foll
18th rows. 89 (95: 101: 107: 113: 121) sts.
Cont straight until work measures 41 (41: 42:
42: 42: 42) cm from cast on edge, ending
with a WS row.
Shape armholes
Keeping patt correct, cast off 4 sts at beg of
next 2 rows. 81 (87: 93: 99: 105: 113) sts.
Dec 1 st at each end of next 5 (5: 7: 7: 9: 11)
rows, then on 1 (2: 2: 3: 3: 3) foll alt rows, and
then on foll 4th row. 67 (71: 73: 77: 79: 83) sts.
Cont straight until armhole measures 21 (22:
22: 23: 24.5: 25.5) cm, ending with a WS row.
Shape shoulders and back neck
Next row (RS): Cast off 4 (4: 5: 5: 5: 5) sts, patt
until there are 9 (10: 10: 11: 12: 13) sts on RH
needle and turn, leaving rem sts on a holder.
Work each side of neck separately.
Dec 1 st at beg of next row, work to end.
Cast off 4 (4: 4: 5: 5: 5) at beg and dec 1 st
at end of next row.
Work 1 row. Cast off rem 3 (4: 4: 4: 5: 6) sts.
With RS facing, rejoin yarn to sts from holder,
cast off centre 41 (43: 43: 45: 45: 47) sts,
patt to end.
Complete to match first side, rev shapings.

Pocket lining (work 2)
Cast on 21 (21: 22: 22: 23: 23) sts using
4 mm (US 6) needles.
Beg with a P row, work 26 rows in rev st st,
Inc 2 sts evenly over the last row.
23 (23: 24: 24: 25: 25) sts.
Leave sts on a holder.

LEFT FRONT
Cast on 56 (59: 62: 65: 68: 72) sts using
4 mm (US 6) needles and work as folls:
Row 1 (RS): K0 (1: 0: 1: 0: 0), (P1, K1) to end.
Row 2: K1, (P1, K1) 6 times, K1, (P1, K1)
to last 0 (1: 0: 1: 0: 0) sts, P0 (1: 0: 1: 0: 0).
Row 3: P0 (1: 0: 1: 0: 0), (K1, P1) to last
14 sts, (P1, K1) to end.
Row 4: K1, (P1, K1) 6 times, K1, (K1, P1)
to last 0 (1: 0: 1: 0: 0) sts, K0 (1: 0: 1: 0: 0).
These 4 rows set the stitches, i.e. the main
part is worked in double moss st, with 13 sts
at front edge worked in moss st and these are
separated with 1 stitch of rev st st which is
worked up the entire front.
Work a further 8 (8: 10: 10: 10: 10) rows,
ending with a WS row.
Cont in patt, dec 1 st at side edge on next
row, then on foll 12th (12th: 12th: 14th:
14th: 14th) row, ending with a RS row.
Work 7 rows ending with a WS row.
Place pocket lining
Next row (RS): Patt 11 (12: 13: 14: 15: 16)
sts, slip next 23 (23: 24: 24: 25: 25) sts onto
a holder and patt across 23 (23: 24: 24: 25:
25) sts of pocket lining, patt to end.
Work 1 (1: 3: 3: 3: 5) rows, ending with a WS row.
Dec 1 st at side edge on next row.
53 (56: 59: 62: 65: 69) sts.
Work 29 rows straight.
Inc 1 st at side edge of next row and 2 foll
18th rows. 56 (59: 62: 65: 68: 72) sts.
Cont straight until left front matches back
to beg of armhole shaping ending with a
WS row.
Shape armhole
Keeping patt correct, cast off 4 sts at beg of
next row. 52 (55: 58: 61: 64: 68) sts.

Work 1 row.

Dec 1 st at armhole edge on next 5 (5: 7: 7: 9: 11) rows, then on 1 (2: 2: 3: 3: 3) foll alt rows, and then on foll 4th row.

45 (47: 48: 50: 51: 53) sts.

Cont straight until 17 (19: 19: 21: 21: 23) rows less have been worked than on back to start of shoulder shaping, ending with a RS row.

Shape neck

Cast off 24 sts at beg of next row.

21 (23: 24: 26: 27: 29) sts.

Dec 1 st at neck edge on next 8 rows, then on 1 (2: 2: 3: 3: 4) foll alt rows, then on foll 4th row. 11 (12: 13: 14: 15: 16) sts.

Work 2 rows, ending with a WS row.

Shape shoulder

Cast off 4 (4: 5: 5: 5: 5) sts at beg of next and 4 (4: 4: 5: 5: 5) at beg of foll alt row.

Work 1 row.

Cast off rem 3 (4: 4: 4: 5: 6) sts.

Pocket tops

With RS facing and using 3 ¾ mm (US 5) needles, slip stitches from holder onto the left needle, rejoin yarn and work 4 rows in pattern.

Cast off in pattern.

Slip stitch pocket tops into place on RS and pocket lining into place on WS.

Mark the positions of 7 buttons on left front, the 2nd to come 52 rows up from cast on edge, the 7th 6 rows down from start of neck shaping, with 3rd, 4th, 5th and 6th spaced evenly between and then the 1st one spaced equal distance below the 2nd.

RIGHT FRONT

Working 6 buttonholes to correspond with positions marked for buttons, complete as given below. Buttonholes worked as folls:

Buttonhole row (RS): Patt 6, cast off next 3 sts, patt to end.

Next row: Patt to where 3 sts cast off, yrn 3 times, patt to end.

Next row: Patt across row, working into back of each of the 3 loops made on previous row.

Cast on 56 (59: 62: 65: 68: 72) sts using 4 mm (US 6) needles and work as folls:

Row 1 (RS): (K1, P1) to last 0 (1: 0: 1: 0: 0), K0 (1: 0: 1: 0: 0)

Row 2: P0 (1: 0: 1: 0: 0), (K1, P1) to last 14 sts, K1, (K1, P1) 6 times, K1.

Row 3: (K1, P1) 7 times, (P1, K1) to last 0 (1: 0: 1: 0: 0) sts, P0 (1: 0: 1: 0: 0).

Row 4: K0 (1: 0: 1: 0: 0), (P1, K1) to last 14 sts, K2, (P1, K1) to end.

These 4 rows set the stitches.

Cont in patt, complete to match left front, reversing all shapings.

SLEEVES (work both the same)

Cast on 75 (77: 79: 81: 83: 85) sts using 4 mm (US 6) needles and work in double moss st as folls:

Row 1 (RS): K1, (P1, K1) to end.

Row 2: P1, (K1, P1) to end.

Row 3: P1, (K1, P1) to end.

Row 4: K1, (P1, K1) to end.

These 4 rows form the patt and are rep throughout.

Work a further 12 (12: 12: 14: 14: 14) rows ending with a WS row.

Cont in patt, dec 1 st at each end of next row and 2 foll 16th (16th: 16th: 18th: 18th: 18th) rows. 69 (71: 73: 75: 77: 79) sts.

Cont in patt until work measures 37.5 (38.5: 39.5: 41: 42: 43) cm from cast on edge, ending with a WS row.

Shape top

Keeping patt correct, cast off 4 sts at beg of next 2 rows. 61 (63: 65: 67: 69: 71) sts.

Dec 1 st at each end of next 3 rows, then on foll alt row. 53 (55: 57: 59: 61: 63) sts.

Work 3 rows, ending with a WS row.

Dec 1 st at each end of next row and every foll 4th row until 39 (39: 41: 55: 57: 59) sts rem.

L, XL & XXL sizes only

Work 5 rows, dec 1 st at each end of next and 1 (2: 2) foll 6th rows, then on every foll 4th row until 45 (47: 47) sts rem.

All sizes

Work 1 row, ending with a WS row.

Dec 1 st at each end of next row and 2 (2: 2: 3: 4: 4) foll alt rows, and then on every foll row until 27 (27: 29: 31: 31: 31) sts rem.

Cast off 3 sts at beg of next 2 rows.

Cast off rem 21 (21: 23: 25: 25: 25) sts.

MAKING UP

Join both shoulder seams using backstitch or mattress st if preferred.

Join side and sleeve seams (but do not sew sleeve into armhole until after washing).

Collar

Cast on 127 (133: 133: 139: 139: 145) sts using 3 ¾ mm (US 5) needles and work in moss st setting stitches as folls:

Row 1 (RS): K1, (P1, K1) to end.

Row 2: Work as row 1.

These 2 rows form moss st and are repeated throughout.

Work a further 4 (4: 6: 6: 8: 8) rows.

Place a maker around the 39th (41st: 41st: 43rd: 43rd: 45th) st in from each end.

Next row (RS)(dec): Patt to 1 st before marker, patt 3tog, patt to 1 st before next marker, patt 3tog, patt to end.

123 (129: 129: 135: 135: 141) sts.

Work 7 rows, ending with a WS row.

Dec as before on next row and foll 8th row.

115 (121: 121: 127: 127: 133) sts.

Work 1 row, ending with a WS row.

Cast off 17 sts at beg of next 2 rows.

Cast off 9 (10: 10: 11: 11: 12) sts at beg of next 4 rows.

Place a marker at each end of last row.

Cast off rem 45 (47: 47: 49: 49: 51) sts.

Positioning ends of the shaped edge of collar halfway across front moss st borders as in photograph, matching centre of collar to centre back neck and markers with shoulder seams, pin and then neatly stitch collar in place around neck edge.

Machine wash all pieces together before completing sewing-up. Set sleeves into armholes. Sew on buttons to correspond with buttonholes.

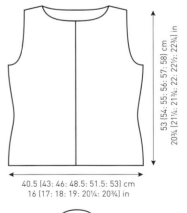

53 [54: 55: 56: 57: 58] cm
20¾ [21¼: 21¾: 22: 22½: 22¾] in

40.5 [43: 46: 48.5: 51.5: 53] cm
16 [17: 18: 19: 20¼: 20¾] in

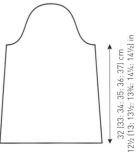

32 [33: 34: 35: 36: 37] cm
12½ [13: 13½: 13¾: 14¼: 14½] in

STEVIE
BOXY GARTER STITCH CADIGAN

Recommendation

Suitable for the knitter with a little experience.
Please see pages 25 & 39 for photographs.

	XS	S	M	L	XL	XXL	
To fit	**81**	**86**	**91**	**97**	**102**	**107**	**cm**
bust	32	34	36	38	40	42	in

Rowan Wool Cotton

      10   11   12   12   13   14 x 50gm

Photographed in Bilberrry

Buttons – 1 large

Needles

1 pair 3 mm (no 11) (US 2/3) needles
1 pair 3¼ mm (no 10) (US 3) needles

Tension

25 sts and 44 rows to 10 cm measured over
garter st, when slightly stretched, using
3¼ mm (US 3) needles.

Tension note: When knitted into a large piece
garter stitch 'drops' and opens up. To ensure
an accurate tension, stretch your square
slightly before measuring.

Special abbreviation:

MP = Make picot: cast on 1 st, cast off 1 st.
(See information page for details)

Pattern note: When knitting fronts, it is
advisable to join in new balls of yarn at side
seam or armhole edge so that front opening
edge remains neat and tidy as there are no
front opening edgings added afterwards.

BACK

Cast on 97 (103: 109: 115: 121: 127) sts
using 3 mm (US 2/3) needles and work
10 rows in garter st, ending with a WS row.
Change to 3¼ mm (US 3) needles and cont
in garter st throughout as folls:
Work 10 rows, ending with a WS row.
Next row (RS)(inc): K3, M1, K to last 3 sts,
M1, K3. 99 (105: 111: 117: 123: 129) sts.
Working all incs as set by last row, inc 1 st at
each end of every foll 20th row until there are
105 (111: 117: 123: 129: 135) sts.
Cont straight until back measures 22 (22: 23:
23: 24: 24) cm, ending with a WS row.

Shape armholes

Cast off 4 (5: 5: 6: 6: 7) sts at beg of next
2 rows. 97 (101: 107: 111: 117: 121) sts.
Next row (RS)(dec): K3, K2tog, K to last 5 sts,
K2tog tbl, K3.
Next row: K3, K2tog tbl, K to last 5 sts,
K2tog, K3.
Working all decs as set by last 2 rows, dec 1
st at each end of next 1 (1: 3: 3: 5: 5) rows,
then on 3 (4: 4: 5: 5: 6) foll alt rows, then on
every foll 4th row until 79 (81: 83: 85: 87: 89)
sts rem.
Cont straight until armhole measures 18 (19:
19: 20: 20: 21) cm, ending with a WS row.

Shape shoulders and back neck

Cast off 7 (7: 7: 7: 8: 8) sts at beg of next
4 rows, then 7 (7: 8: 8: 7: 7) sts at beg of
foll 2 rows. 37 (39: 39: 41: 43: 45) sts.
Cast off.

LEFT FRONT

Cast on 54 (57: 60: 63: 66: 69) sts using 3
mm (US 2/3) needles and work as folls:
Next row (RS): Knit.
Next row: MP, K to end.
Next row: K to last 20 sts, K2tog, yon, K to
end.
Next row: Knit.
These 4 rows form garter st with eyelet patt
and picot trim edging.
Work a further 6 rows as set, ending with a
WS row.

Change to 3¼ mm (US 3) needles and cont
in patt as folls:
Work 10 rows, ending with a WS row.
Next row (RS)(inc): K3, M1, patt to end.
55 (58: 61: 64: 67: 70) sts.
Working all incs as set by last row, inc 1 st at
beg of every foll 20th row until there are 58
(61: 64: 67: 70: 73) sts.
Cont straight until left front measures same
as back to beg of armhole shaping, ending
with a WS row.

Shape armhole

Keeping patt correct, cast off 4 (5: 5: 6: 6: 7)
sts at beg of next row.
51 (53: 56: 58: 61: 63) sts.
Next row (RS)(dec): K3, K2tog, patt to end.
Next row: Patt to last 5 sts, K2tog, K3.
Working all decs as set by last 2 rows, dec
1 st at armhole edge of next 1 (1: 3: 3: 5: 5)
rows, then on 3 (4: 4: 5: 5: 6) foll alt rows,
then on every foll 4th row until 45 (46: 47: 48:
49: 50) sts rem.
Cont straight until left front measures same
as back to start of shoulder shaping, ending
with a WS row.

Shape shoulder

Cast off 7 (7: 7: 7: 8: 8) sts at beg of next
and foll alt row.
Work 1 row.
Cast off 7 (7: 8: 8: 7: 7) sts at beg of
next row.
24 (25: 25: 26: 26: 27) sts.
Work 1 row.
Break yarn, leaving rem sts on a holder for
neckband.

RIGHT FRONT

Cast on 54 (57: 60: 63: 66: 69) sts using
3 mm (US 2/3) needles and work as folls:
Next row (RS): Knit.
Next row: Knit.
Next row: MP, K until there are 18 sts on
RH needle, yon, K2tog tbl, K to end.
Next row: Knit.
These 4 rows form garter st with eyelet patt
and picot trim edging.

Work a further 6 rows as set, ending with a WS row.

Change to 3¼ mm (US 3) needles and cont in patt as folls:

Work 10 rows, ending with a WS row.

Next row (RS)(inc): Patt to last 3 sts, M1, K3. 55 (58: 61: 64: 67: 70) sts.

Working all incs as set by last row, inc 1 st at end of every foll 20th row until there are 58 (61: 64: 67: 70: 73) sts.

Work 1 (5: 5: 9: 9: 13) rows straight, ending with a WS row.

Next row (RS)(buttonhole row): Patt until there are 8 sts on RH needle, cast off 3 sts, patt to end and back, casting-on 3 sts over those cast-off on previous row.

Complete to match left front, reversing all shapings.

Do not break yarn at neck edge, join in a new ball of yarn to complete right front, saving the first ball of yarn to work neckband.

SLEEVES (both alike)
Cuff (knitted from side to side)
Cast on 13 (13: 14: 14: 15: 15) sts using 3 mm (US 2/3) needles and work as folls:

Next row (RS): MP, K to last 4 sts, K2tog tbl, yon, K2.

Next row: Knit.

Next row: MP, K to end.

Next row: Knit.

These 4 rows form garter st with eyelet patt and picot trim edging.

Rep these 4 rows a further 27 (28: 29: 30: 31: 32) times, ending with a WS row.

Cast off, but do not break yarn.

UPPER SLEEVE
With RS facing, and using 3¼ mm (US 3) needles, pick up and knit 69 (71: 73: 75: 77: 79) sts along straight edge of cuff.

Work 23 rows in garter st, ending with a WS row.

Next row (RS)(inc): K3, M1, K to last 3 sts, M1, K3. 71 (73: 75: 77: 79: 81) sts.

Working all incs as set by last row, cont in garter st, inc 1 st at each end of every foll 24th (26th: 20th: 20th: 20th: 14th) row to 77 (79: 83: 81: 81: 87) sts, then on every foll – (·: ·: 22nd: 22nd: 16th) row until there are – (·: ·: 85: 87: 93) sts.

Cont straight until sleeve measures 27 (28: 28.5: 29.5: 30: 31) cm from pick-up row, ending with a WS row.

Shape sleevehead
Cast off 4 (5: 5: 6: 6: 7) sts at beg of next 2 rows.

69 (69: 73: 73: 75: 79) sts.

Dec 1 st at each end of next 3 (3: 5: 5: 5: 7) rows, then on foll alt row.

61 (61: 61: 61: 63: 63) sts.

Work 3 rows, ending with a WS row.

Dec 1 st at each end of next row and 3 foll 4th rows, then on every foll 6th row until 49 (49: 49: 47: 49: 49) sts rem.

Work 3 rows, ending with a WS row.

Dec 1 st at each end of next row and 1 (2: 1: 1: 1: 1) foll 4th rows, then on 5 (5: 6: 5: 5: 6) foll alt rows, then on every foll row until 29 (27: 27: 27: 29: 27) sts rem, ending with a WS row.

Cast off 3 sts at beg of next 2 rows.

Cast off rem 23 (21: 21: 21: 23: 21) sts.

MAKING UP
Press as described on information page.

Join both shoulder seams using backstitch or mattress stitch if preferred.

Neckband
With RS facing and using 3 mm (US 2/3) needles, patt across 24 (25: 25: 26: 26: 27) sts from right front holder, pick up and knit 37 (39: 39: 41: 41: 43) sts from back, then patt across 24 (25: 25: 26: 26: 27) sts from left front holder.

85 (89: 89: 93: 93: 97) sts.

Patt 12 rows, ending with a **RS** row.

Cast off knitwise (on WS).

Join side and sleeve seams.

Set sleeves in to armholes using the set-in method.

Sew on button to correspond with buttonhole

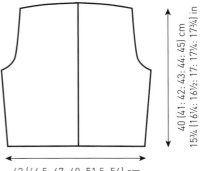

42 (44.5: 47: 49: 51.5: 54) cm
16½ (17½: 18½: 19¼: 20¼: 21¼) in

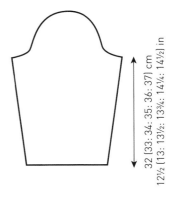

ROSE
SWEATER WITH SPLIT COLLAR & GENEROUS BACK NECK

Recommendation
Suitable for the knitter with a little experience.
Please see pages 26 & 27 for photographs.

	XS	S	M	L	XL	XXL	
To fit	**81**	**86**	**91**	**97**	**102**	**109**	**cm**
bust	32	34	36	38	40	43	in

Rowan Handknit cotton
| 12 | 13 | 14 | 15 | 16 | 17 | x 50gm |
Photographed in Thunder

Needles
1 pair 3¾ mm (no 9) (US 5) needles
1 pair 4 mm (no 8) (US 6) needles

Tension
20 sts and 28 rows to 10 cm measured over
reverse st st using 4 mm (US 6) needles.

Special abbreviation
MP = Make picot: cast on 1 st, cast off 1 st.
(See information page for details)

BACK
**Lower edging (knitted from side to side)
Cast on 14 (15: 16: 17: 18) sts using 3¾ mm
(US 5) needles.
Knit 2 rows.
Shape side edge
Next row (RS): MP, K until 6 (7: 8: 9: 10)
sts on right needle, wrap next stitch (by
slipping next st to right needle, taking
yarn to opposite side of work between
needles and then slipping same st back
onto left needle – when working back across
sts, work the wrapped loop tog with the
wrapped st), turn and K to end.
Next row: MP, K until 10 (11: 12: 13: 14) sts
on right needle, wrap next stitch, turn and K
to end.
Keeping picot edging correct as set, cont in
garter st for a further 128 (132: 142: 148:
156) rows, ending with a WS row.
Shape side edge
Next row: MP, K until 10 (11: 12: 13: 14) sts
on right needle, wrap next stitch, turn and K
to end.
Next row: MP, K until 6 (7: 8: 9: 10) sts on
right needle, wrap next stitch, turn and K
to end.
Knit 2 rows.
Cast off, but do not break yarn.
Upper back
With RS of lower edging facing and using
4 mm (US 6) needles, pick up and knit 85
(89: 95: 99: 105) sts evenly along the top
(straight) edge of
peplum and knit 1 row, ending with a WS row.
Beg with a P row, cont in reverse st st as folls:
Work 2 (2: 4: 4: 4) rows, ending with a
WS row.
Next row (RS) (dec): P2, P2tog tbl, P to last
4 sts, P2tog, P2.
83 (87: 93: 97: 103) sts.
Work 3 rows, ending with a WS row.
Dec as before on next row and every foll
4th row until 77 (81: 87: 91: 97) sts rem.
Work 9 (11: 11: 11: 11) rows, ending with
a WS row. **

Next row (RS)(inc): P2, M1P, P to last 2 sts,
M1P, P2.
79 (83: 89: 93: 99) sts.
Work 9 rows, ending with a WS row.
Inc as before on next row and foll 10th row,
then on every foll 8th row until there are
87 (91: 97: 101: 107) sts.
Cont until work measures 32 (33: 33:
33: 34) cm from lower edge, ending
with a WS row.
Shape raglans
Cast off 4 sts at beg of next 2 rows.
79 (83: 89: 93: 99) sts.
Work 3 rows.
Next row (RS) (dec): P2, P2tog tbl, P to last
4 sts, P2tog, P2.
77 (81: 87: 91: 97) sts.
Work 3 rows.
Dec as before on next row and every foll
4th row until 55 (61: 71: 73: 83) sts rem.
Work 1 row, ending with a WS row.
Dec as before on next row and every foll alt
row until 49 (51: 51: 53: 55) sts rem.
Work 1 row.
Cast off.

FRONT
Work as given for back from ** to **.
Next row (RS)(inc): P2, M1P, P to last 2 sts,
M1P, P2.
79 (83: 89: 93: 99) sts.
Work 9 rows, ending with a WS row.
Inc as before on next row and foll 10th row,
then on foll 8th row.
85 (89: 95: 99: 105) sts.
Work 3 rows, ending with a WS row.
Divide for front neck
Next row (RS): P37 (39: 42: 44: 47) sts,
and leave these on a holder for left front, K11,
P37 (39: 42: 44: 47) sts.
Work on these 48 (50: 53: 55: 58) sts for
right front.
Next row: Knit.
Next row (RS): MP, K until 11 sts on right
needle, P to end.
Next row: Knit.

Next row (inc): MP, K until 11 sts on right needle, P to last 2 sts, M1P, P2.
49 (51: 54: 56: 59) sts.
Knit 1 row.
Next row (RS): MP, K until 11 sts on right needle, P to end.
Knit 1 row.
Rep these 2 rows until right front matches back to armhole shaping, ending with a **RS** row.

Shape raglan
Cast off 4 sts at beg of next row.
45 (47: 50: 52: 55) sts
Work 2 rows.
Next row (RS)(dec): Work to last 4 sts, P2tog, P2.
Work 3 rows.
Dec as before on next row and then on every foll 4th row until 33 (36: 41: 42: 47) sts rem.
Work 1 row.
Dec as before on next row and on every foll alt row until 30 (31: 31: 32: 33) sts rem.
Work 1 row, ending with a WS row.
Do not break yarn. Leave yarn attached for collar.
Leave sts on a spare needle.
With **WS** facing, cast on 11 sts, rejoin yarn to sts for left front and K to end.
48 (50: 53: 55: 58) sts.
Keeping shaping correct, complete as for right front, reversing shapings and working a picot at beg of every **WS** row.
Break yarn and leave sts on a spare needle.

SLEEVES (both alike)
Lower edging (knitted from side to side)
Cast on 14 (15: 16: 17: 18) sts using 3¾ mm (US 5) needles.
Knit 2 rows.
Shape side edge
Next row (RS): MP, K until 6 (7: 8: 9: 10) sts on right needle, wrap next stitch, turn and K to end.
Next row: MP, K until 10 (11: 12: 13: 14) sts on right needle, wrap next stitch, turn and K to end.
Keeping picot edging correct, cont in garter st for a further 80 (88: 96: 104: 112) rows, ending with a WS row.
Shape side edge
Next row: MP, K until 10 (11: 12: 13: 14) sts on right needle, wrap next stitch, turn and K to end.

Next row: MP, K until 6 (7: 8: 9: 10) sts on right needle, wrap next stitch, turn and K to end.
Knit 2 rows.
Cast off, but do not break yarn.

UPPER SLEEVE
With RS of lower edging facing and using 4 mm (US 6) needles, pick up and knit 49 (53: 57: 61: 65) sts evenly along the top (straight) edge of peplum and knit 1 row, ending with a WS row.
Beg with a P row, cont in reverse st st as folls:
Work 4 rows.
Next row (RS) (dec): P2, P2tog tbl, P to last 4 sts, P2tog, P2.
47 (51: 55: 59: 63) sts.
Work 3 (3: 5: 5: 5) rows, ending with a WS row.
Dec as before on next row and foll 4th row.
43 (47: 51: 55: 59) sts.
Work 13 rows, ending with a WS row.
Next row (RS)(inc): P2, M1P, P to last 2 sts, M1P, P2.
45 (49: 53: 57: 61) sts.
Work 9 rows, ending with a WS row.
Inc as before on next row and 2 foll 10th rows,
then on every foll 8th row until there are 59 (63: 67: 71: 75) sts.
Cont straight until sleeve measures 42 (43: 44: 45: 46) cm, ending with a WS row.
Shape raglan
Cast off 4 sts at beg of next 2 rows.
51 (55: 59: 63: 67) sts.
Work 2 rows.
Next row (RS) (dec): P2, P2tog tbl, P to last 4 sts, P2tog, P2.
Work 3 rows.
Dec as before on next row and every foll 4th row until 33 (39: 45: 47: 55) sts rem.
Work 1 row, ending with a WS row.
Dec as before on next row and every foll alt row until 15 (17: 17: 19: 19) sts rem.
Work 1 row, ending with a WS row.
Cast off.

MAKING UP
Press all pieces using a warm iron over a damp cloth.
Join raglan seams using back stitch or mattress stitch if preferred.

Collar
With RS facing and using 3¾ mm (US 5) needles, work across 30 (31: 31: 32: 33) sts from right front as folls: K12 (11: 11: 12: 11), (P1, K1) to last 2 sts, P2tog, pick up and knit 14 (15: 15: 17: 17) across top of right sleeve, 47 (49: 49: 51: 55) sts across back, then 14 (15: 15: 17: 17) sts across top of left sleeve, work across 30 (31: 31: 32: 33) sts from left front as folls: P2tog, (K1, P1) to last 12 (11: 11: 12: 11) sts, K12 (11: 11: 12: 11).
133 (139: 139: 147: 153) sts.
Next row (WS of garment, RS of collar): K11, rib to last 11 sts, K11.
Cont as set until collar measures 13 (14: 14: 15: 16) cm.
Cast off in pattern.
Join side and sleeve seams.
Neatly slip stitch cast-on sts at base of left front neck in to place behind the right front.

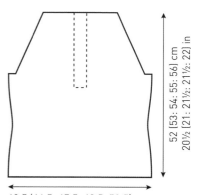

52 (53: 54: 55: 56) cm
20½ (21: 21½: 21½: 22) in

42.5 (44.5: 47.5: 49.5: 52.5) cm
16½ (17½ : 18½ : 19½ : 20½) in

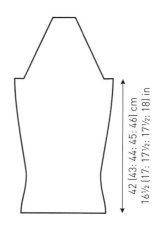

42 (43: 44: 45: 46) cm
16½ (17: 17½: 17½: 18) in

FRANKIE
BOYFRIEND CARDIGAN WITH DEEP RAGLANS

Recommendation
Suitable for the knitter with a little experience.
Please see pages 30 & 31 for photographs.

	XS	S	M	L	XL	XXL	
To fit	**81**	**86**	**91**	**97**	**102**	**109**	cm
bust	32	34	36	38	40	43	in

Rowan Classic Pima Cotton DK

10 11 11 12 12 13 x50gm
Photographed in Badger

Buttons · 3

Needles
1 pair 3 ¼mm (no 10) (US 3) needles
1 pair 3 ¾mm (no 9) (US 5) needles

Tension
23 sts and 30 rows to 10 cm measured over
stocking stitch using 3 ¾mm (US 5) needles.

Pattern note: When knitting fronts, it is
advisable to join in new balls of yarn at side
seam or armhole edge so that front opening
edge remains neat and tidy as there are no
front opening edgings added afterwards.

BACK
Cast on 111 (117: 123: 129: 135: 143) sts
using 3 ¾mm (US 5) needles.
Row 1 (RS): K1 (1: 1: 1: 1: 2), (P1, K2) to
last 2 (2: 2: 2: 2: 3) sts, P1, K1 (1: 1: 1: 1: 2).
Row 2: P1 (1: 1: 1: 1: 2), (K1, P2) to last 2
(2: 2: 2: 2: 3) sts, K1, P1 (1: 1: 1: 1: 2).
These 2 rows form rib.
Work in rib for 18 (18: 20: 20: 22: 22) rows
more, ending with a WS row.
Beg with a K row, work in st st until back
measures 41 cm, ending with a WS row.
Shape raglan armholes
Cast off 6 sts at beg of next 2 rows.
99 (105: 111: 117: 123: 131) sts.
Work 4 rows.
Next row (dec) (RS): K1, K3tog, K to last
4 sts, K3tog tbl, K1.
95 (101: 107: 113: 119: 127) sts.
Work 5 rows.
Dec 2 sts as before at each end of next and
7 (6: 6: 5: 5: 2) foll 6th rows, then on 3 (5: 6:
8: 9: 14) foll 4th rows.
51 (53: 55: 57: 59: 59) sts.
Work 3 rows, ending with a WS row.
Cast off.

POCKET LININGS (make 2)
Cast on 27 (27: 29: 29: 31: 31) sts using
3 ¾mm (US 5) needles.
Beg with a K row, work 34 rows in st st.
Leave sts on a holder.

LEFT FRONT
Cast on 64 (67: 70: 73: 76: 80) sts using
3 ¾mm (US 5) needles.
Row 1 (RS): K1 (1: 1: 1: 1: 2), (P1, K2) to
last 15 sts, P to end.
Row 2: K15, (P2, K1) to last 1 (1: 1: 1: 1: 2)
sts, P1 (1: 1: 1: 1: 2).
Row 3: K1 (1: 1: 1: 1: 2), (P1, K2) to last 15
sts, P1, K14.
Row 4: P14, K1, (P2, K1) to last 1 (1: 1: 1: 1:
2) sts, P1 (1: 1: 1: 1: 2).
These 4 rows set the sts – front opening edge
15 sts in ridge patt with all other sts in rib.

Cont as set for 16 (16: 18: 18: 20: 20) rows
more, ending with a WS row.
Next row (RS): K to last 15 sts, patt to end.
Next row: Patt 15 sts, P to end.
These 2 rows set the sts for rest of left front
– front opening edge 15 sts still in ridge patt
with all other sts now in st st.
Cont as set for 22 rows, ending with a WS row.
Place pocket
Next row (RS): K9 (10: 11: 12: 13: 14), slip
next 27 (27: 29: 29: 31: 31) sts onto a holder
and, in their place, K across 27 (27: 29: 29:
31: 31) sts of first pocket lining, patt to end.
Cont straight until 26 rows less have been
worked than on back to beg of raglan
armhole shaping, ending with a WS row.
Shape front slope
Next row (dec) (RS): K to last 17 sts, K2tog
tbl, patt to end. 63 (66: 69: 72: 75: 79) sts.
Working all front slope decreases as set by
last row, cont as folls:
Work 3 rows.
Dec 1 st as before at front slope edge of next
and 5 foll 4th rows.
57 (60: 63: 66: 69: 73) sts.
Work 1 row, ending with a WS row.
Shape raglan armhole
Keeping patt correct, cast off 6 sts at beg of
next row. 51 (54: 57: 60: 63: 67) sts.
Work 1 row.
Dec 1 st as before at front slope edge of next
and 8 (10: 11: 13: 14: 13) foll 4th rows, then
on 4 (3: 3: 2: 2: 3) foll 6th rows and **at same
time,** working all raglan armhole decreases in
same way as given for back raglan armhole,
dec 2 sts at raglan armhole edge of 5th and 8
(7: 7: 6: 6: 3) foll 6th rows, then on 1 (3: 4: 6:
7: 12) foll 4th rows. 18 sts.
Work 3 rows, ending with a WS row.
Next row (RS): K3tog, patt to end. 16 sts.
Work 1 row.
Next row: P2tog, patt to end. 15 sts.
Cont in ridge patt on these 15 sts only for a
further 20 (20.5: 21: 21.5: 22: 22) cm (for back
neck border extension), ending with a WS row.
Cast off.

RIGHT FRONT

Cast on 64 (67: 70: 73: 76: 80) sts using 3 ¾mm (US 5) needles.

Row 1 (RS): P15, (K2, P1) to last 1 (1: 1: 1: 1: 2) sts, K1 (1: 1: 1: 1: 2).

Row 2: P1 (1: 1: 1: 1: 2), (K1, P2) to last 15 sts, K15.

Row 3: K14, P1, (K2, P1) to last 1 (1: 1: 1: 1: 2) sts, K1 (1: 1: 1: 1: 2).

Row 4: P1 (1: 1: 1: 1: 2), (K1, P2) to last 15 sts, K1, P14.

These 4 rows set the sts – front opening edge 15 sts in ridge patt with all other sts in rib.

Cont as set for 16 (16: 18: 18: 20: 20) rows more, ending with a WS row.

Next row (RS): Patt 15 sts, K to end.

Next row: P to last 15 sts, patt to end.

These 2 rows set the sts for rest of right front – front opening edge 15 sts still in ridge patt with all other sts now in st st.

Cont as set for 4 (4: 2: 2: 0: 0) rows, ending after ridge patt row 2 and with a WS row.

Next row (buttonhole row) (RS): K5, cast off next 4 sts (to make a buttonhole – cast on 4 sts over these cast-off sts on next row), patt to end.

Working a further 2 buttonholes in this way on 32nd and foll 32nd row and noting that no further reference will be made to buttonholes, cont as folls:

Work 17 (17: 19: 19: 21: 21) rows, ending with a WS row.

Place pocket

Next row (RS): Patt 28 (30: 30: 32: 32: 35) sts, slip next 27 (27: 29: 29: 31: 31) sts onto a holder and, in their place, K across 27 (27: 29: 29: 31: 31) sts of second pocket lining, K to end.

Cont straight until 26 rows less have been worked than on back to beg of raglan armhole shaping, ending with a WS row.

Shape front slope

Next row (dec) (RS): Patt 15 sts, K2tog, K to end. 63 (66: 69: 72: 75: 79) sts.

Working all front slope decreases as set by last row, complete to match left front, reversing shapings.

Sleeves (both alike)
Cuff

Cast on 15 (15: 16: 16: 17: 17) sts using 3 ¾mm (US 5) needles.

Row 1 (RS): Knit.

Rows 2 and 3: Purl.

Row 4: Knit.

These 4 rows form ridge patt.

Rep last 4 rows 18 (19: 19: 20: 20: 21) times more, then rows 1 and 2 again, ending with a WS row.

Cast off, but do **NOT** break yarn.

Main section

With RS facing and using 3 ¾mm (US 5) needles, pick up and knit 81 (83: 85: 87: 89: 91) sts along row-end edge of cuff.

Beg with a P row, work in st st as folls:

Work 7 rows, ending with a WS row.

Next row (inc) (RS): K3, M1, K to last 3 sts, M1, K3. 83 (85: 87: 89: 91: 93) sts.

Work 5 rows.

Inc 1 st as before at each end of next and 4 (6: 7: 9: 10: 12) foll 4th rows, then on foll 11 (9: 8: 6: 5: 3) alt rows.

115 (117: 119: 121: 123: 125) sts.

Work 3 rows, ending with a WS row.

Shape raglan

Cast off 6 sts at beg of next 2 rows. 103 (105: 107: 109: 111: 113) sts.

Next row (RS)(dec): K1, K3tog, K to last 4 sts, K3tog tbl, K1. 99 (101: 103: 105: 107: 109) sts.

Work 1 row.

Dec 2 sts as before on next and foll 7 (6: 6: 5: 5: 4) alt rows, then on every foll 4th row until 23 (25: 23: 25: 23: 25) sts rem.

Work 1 row, ending with a WS row.

Left sleeve only

Work 1 row.

Cast off 4 (5: 4: 5: 4: 5) sts at beg of next row, then 6 sts at beg of foll 2 alt rows, ending with a WS row, **and at same time** dec 2 sts as before at beg of 2nd of these rows.

Right sleeve only

Cast off 4 (5: 4: 5: 4: 5) sts at beg of next row, then 6 sts at beg of foll 2 alt rows and **at same time** dec 2 sts as before at end of 3rd of these rows.

Work 1 row, ending with a WS row.

Both sleeves

Cast off rem 5 (6: 5: 6: 5: 6) sts.

MAKING UP

Pin out pieces and press carefully following instructions on ball band.

Pocket tops (both alike)

Slip 27 (27: 29: 29: 31: 31) sts from pocket holder onto 3 ¼mm (US 3) needles and rejoin yarn with **RS** facing.

Beg with a K row, work in st st for 5 rows, ending with a RS row.

Cast off purlwise (on **WS**).

Sew pocket linings in place on inside, then neatly sew down ends of pocket tops, allowing them to roll to RS as in photograph. Join all raglan seams. Join cast-off ends of back neck border extensions, then neatly sew one edge in place to top of sleeves and back neck.

Join side and sleeve seams.

Sew on buttons.

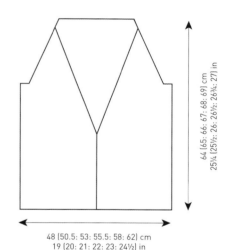

64 (65: 66: 67: 68: 69) cm
25¼ (25½: 26: 26½: 26¾: 27) in

48 (50.5: 53: 55.5: 58: 62) cm
19 (20: 21: 22: 23: 24½) in

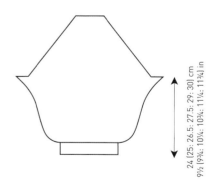

24 (25: 26.5: 27.5: 29: 30) cm
9½ (9¾: 10¼: 10¾: 11½: 11¾) in

PURE
RAGLAN SWEATER WITH FLOUNCE HEM & SLASHED NECK

Recommendation
Suitable for the novice knitter.
Please see pages 50 & 51 for photographs.

	XS	S	M	L	XL	XXL	
To fit	**81**	**86**	**91**	**97**	**102**	**109**	cm
bust	32	34	36	38	40	43	in

Rowan Classic Bamboo Soft
11   11   12   13   14   15   x 50gm
Photographed in Balsamic

Needles
1 pair 3 ¼mm (no 10) (US 3) needles
1 pair 3 ¾mm (no 9) (US 5) needles

Tension
24 sts and 30 rows to 10 cm measured over using 3 ¾mm (US 5) needles

Tension note: The Bamboo Soft yarn relaxes after steaming. This opens the knitting and changes the tension by approximately one stitch in the width but does not affect the rows (23 sts and 30 rows). Therefore your knitting, before steaming, should have a tension of 24 sts and 30 rows to 10 cm (over st st). Allowances have been made within the pattern for this change (see size diagram for after relaxing measurements).

Special Abbreviations
Right Dec: Sl 1, K1, psso, slip st now on right needle back onto left needle, lift 2nd st on left needle over this st and off left needle, and then slip rem st back onto right needle.
Left dec: Sl 1, K2tog, psso.

BACK
Cast on 270 (290: 310: 330: 338: 374) sts using 3 ¾mm (US 5) needles and work lower flounce as folls:
Row 1 (dec) (RS): *K2, lift first st over 2nd st (1 st dec); rep from * to end.
135 (145: 155: 165: 169: 187) sts.
Row 2: Purl.
Beg with a K row, cont in st st until work measures 14 (14: 14: 15: 15: 15) cm, ending with a WS row.
Change to 3 ¼mm (US 3) needles.
Next row (dec) (RS): K1 (1: 0: 0: 2: 0), (K1, K3tog, K3, K3tog, K1) to last 2 (1: 1: 0: 2: 0) sts, K2 (1: 1: 0: 2: 0).
87 (93: 99: 105: 109: 119) sts.
Cont in st st shaping sides as folls:
Work 7 rows.
Change to 3 ¾mm (US 5) needles.
Work 2 rows more, ending with a WS row.
Next row (inc) (RS): K2, M1, K to last 2 sts, M1, K2.
89 (95: 101: 107: 111: 121) sts.
Work 9 rows.
Inc 1 st as before at each end of next and 4 foll 10th rows.
99 (105: 111: 117: 121: 131) sts.
Work straight until back measures 36 (37: 37: 39: 39: 39) cm, ending with a WS row.

Shape raglan armholes
Cast off 5 (6: 5: 6: 6: 6) sts at beg of next 2 rows.
89 (93: 101: 105: 109: 119) sts.
Work 2 rows.
Next row (dec) (RS): K2, **right dec**, K to last 5 sts, **left dec**, K2. 85 (89: 97: 101: 105: 115) sts.
Work 5 rows.
Dec 2 sts as before at each end of next and 1 (2: 2: 3: 5: 4) foll 6th rows, then on 8 (7: 8: 7: 5: 7) foll 4th rows.
45 (49: 53: 57: 61: 67) sts.
Work 3 rows, ending with a WS row.
Leave rem sts on a holder.

FRONT
Work as given for back.

SLEEVES (work both the same)
Cast on 49 (51: 53: 55: 57: 59) sts using 3 ¼mm (US 3) needles.
Beg with a K row, cont in st st shaping sides as folls:
Work 10 rows, ending with a WS row.
Change to 3 ¾mm (US 5) needles.
Work 2 (2: 2: 2: 4: 4) rows.
Next row (inc) (RS): K2, M1, K to last 2 sts, M1, K2.
51 (53: 55: 57: 59: 61) sts.
Work 9 rows, ending with a WS row.
Inc 1 st as before at each end of next and every foll 10th row to 67 (69: 65: 67: 65: 67) sts, then on every foll 12th row until there are 71 (73: 75: 77: 79: 81) sts.
Work straight until sleeve measures 41 (42: 43: 44: 45: 46) cm, ending with a WS row.

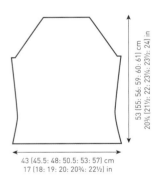

43 (45.5: 48: 50.5: 53: 57) cm
17 (18: 19: 20: 20¾: 22½) in

53 (55: 56: 59: 60: 61) cm
20¾ (21½: 22: 23¾: 23¾: 24) in

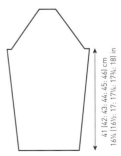

41 (42: 43: 44: 45: 46) cm
16¼ (16½: 17: 17¾: 17¾: 18) in

Continued on following page…

DAISY
NEAT FITTING CARDIGAN WITH CONTRASTING TRIMS

Recommendation

Suitable for the knitter with a little experience.
Please see pages 34 & 35 for photographs.

	XS	S	M	L	XL	XXL	
To fit	**81**	**86**	**91**	**97**	**102**	**109**	**cm**
bust	32	34	36	38	40	43	in

Rowan Classic Pima Cotton DK

| Main colour | 6 | 7 | 7 | 8 | 8 | 9 | x 50g |
| Contrast | 1 | 1 | 1 | 1 | 1 | 1 | x 50g |

Photographed in Lozenge & Badger

Buttons - 6

Needles

1 pair 3mm (no 11) (US 2/3) needles
1 pair 3 ¼ mm (no 10) (US 3) needles

Tension

26 sts and 34 rows to 10 cm measured over
stocking stitch using 3 ¼ mm (US 3) needles.

BACK

Cast on 97 (103: 109: 117: 123: 133) sts
using 3 ¼ mm (US 3) needles and **main yarn**.
Knit 3 rows.
Row 4 (WS): K1 (0: 1: 1: 0: 1), *P1, K1; rep from
* to last 0 (1: 0: 0: 1: 0) st, P0 (1: 0: 0: 1: 0).
Row 5: As row 4.
Rows 4 and 5 form moss st.
Work in moss st for 5 (5: 7: 7: 9: 9) rows
more, ending with a WS row.
Dec 1 st at each end of next row and 2 foll
6th rows.
91 (97: 103: 111: 117: 127) sts.
Work 5 (5: 3: 3: 1: 1) rows, ending with
a WS row.
Shaping side seams at same time, now work
in textured stripe patt as folls:
Row 1 (RS): (K2, K2tog) 1 (1: 0: 0: 0: 0)
times, K to last 4 (4: 0: 0: 0: 0) sts, (K2tog
tbl, K2) 1 (1: 0: 0: 0: 0) times.
Row 2: Purl.
Row 3: (K2, K2tog) 0 (0: 1: 1: 0: 0) times, K
to last 0 (0: 4: 4: 0: 0) sts, (K2tog tbl, K2) 0
(0: 1: 1: 0: 0) times.
Row 4: Purl.
Row 5: (K2, K2tog) 0 (0: 0: 0: 1: 1) times, K
to last 0 (0: 0: 0: 4: 4) sts, (K2tog tbl, K2) 0
(0: 0: 0: 1: 1) times.
Row 6: Purl.

Rows 7 to 11: As rows 1 to 5. 87 (93: 99:
107: 113: 123) sts.
Row 12 (WS): K0 (1: 0: 0: 1: 0), *P1, K1; rep from
* to last 1 (0: 1: 1: 0: 1) st, P1 (0: 1: 1: 0: 1).
Row 13: (Work 2 tog) 1 (1: 0: 0: 0: 0) times,
K0 (0: 1: 0: 0: 0), *P1, K1; rep from * to last
3 (2: 1: 1: 0: 1) sts, P1 (0: 1: 1: 0: 1), (work 2
tog) 1 (1: 0: 0: 0: 0) times.
85 (91: 99: 107: 113: 123) sts.
Row 14: K1 (0: 0: 0: 1: 0), *P1, K1; rep from
* to last 0 (1: 1: 1: 0: 1) st, P0 (1: 1: 1: 0: 1).
These 14 rows form patt and beg side seam
shaping.
Working all side seam decreases as set, cont
in patt, dec 1 st at each end of 5th (5th: next:
next: 3rd: 3rd) and 0 (0: 1: 1: 1: 1) foll 6th row.
83 (89: 95: 103: 109: 119) sts.
Work 19 rows, ending with a WS row.
Next row (RS): Patt 2 sts, M1, patt to last
2 sts, M1, patt 2 sts.
85 (91: 97: 105: 111: 121) sts.
Working all side seam increases as set by
last row, inc 1 st at each end of 6th (6th:
8th: 8th: 6th: 6th) and 1 (1: 0: 0: 0: 0) foll
6th row, then on 5 (5: 6: 6: 6: 6) foll 8th
rows, taking inc sts into patt.
99 (105: 111: 119: 125: 135) sts.
Work 11 (11: 9: 9: 9: 9) rows, ending after
patt row 4 (4: 8: 8: 8: 8) and with a WS row.

Pure — Continued from previous page...

Shape raglan

Cast off 5 (6: 5: 6: 6: 6) sts at beg of next 2 rows.
61 (61: 65: 65: 67: 69) sts.
Work 2 rows, ending with a WS row.
Next row (dec) (RS): K2, **right dec**, K to last
5 sts, **left dec**, K2.
57 (57: 61: 61: 63: 65) sts.
Work 5 rows, ending with a WS row.
Dec 2 sts as before as each end of next and
1 (2: 2: 5: 7: 8) foll 6th rows, then on 8 (7: 8: 4:
2: 1) foll 4th rows. 17 (17: 17: 21: 23: 25) sts.

Work 3 rows, ending with a WS row.
Leave rem sts on a holder.

MAKING UP

Pin the pieces out, and **steam** gently without
allowing the iron to touch the yarn.
Join three raglan seams leaving the left back
raglan seam open.

Neck edging

With RS facing and using 3 ¼mm (US 3)
needles, work across stitches on holder on

left sleeve as folls: K to last 2 sts, K2tog, work
across front stitches as folls: K2tog, K to last
2 sts, K2tog, work across right sleeve stitches
as folls: K2tog, K to last 2 sts, K2tog, work
across back stitches as folls: K2tog, K to last 2
sts, K2tog.
117 (125: 147: 133: 161: 177) sts.
Beg with a knit row, work 4 rows in rev st st.
Cast off knitwise (on WS).
Join rem raglan and neckband seam.
Join side and sleeve seams.

Shape armholes

Keeping patt correct, cast off 4 (4: 4: 4: 5: 5) sts at beg of next 2 rows.
91 (97: 103: 111: 115: 125) sts.
Dec 1 st at each end of next 4 (5: 5: 6: 6: 8) rows, then on foll 3 (2: 3: 3: 3: 3) alt rows, and then on 0 (1: 1: 1: 1: 1) foll 4th row.
77 (81: 85: 91: 95: 101) sts.
Work 46 (47: 45: 46: 50: 52) rows, ending after patt row 6 (10: 14: 2: 6: 10) and with a WS row.

Shape shoulders and back neck

Cast off 6 (6: 6: 7: 7: 8) sts at beg of next 2 rows. 65 (69: 73: 77: 81: 85) sts.
Next row (RS): Cast off 6 (6: 6: 7: 7: 8) sts, patt until there are 9 (10: 11: 11: 12: 12) sts on right needle and turn, leaving rem sts on a holder.
Work each side of neck separately.
Cast off 4 sts at beg of next row.
Cast off rem 5 (6: 7: 7: 8: 8) sts.
With RS facing, rejoin yarn to rem sts, cast off centre 35 (37: 39: 41: 43: 45) sts, patt to end.
Complete to match first side, reversing shapings.

POCKET LININGS (make 2)

Cast on 21 (21: 23: 23: 25: 25) sts using 3 ¼ mm (US 3) needles and **contrast yarn.**
Beg with a K row, work 25 rows in st st, ending with a **RS** row.
Leave sts on a spare needle.

LEFT FRONT

Cast on 54 (57: 60: 64: 67: 72) sts using 3 ¼ mm (US 3) needles and **main yarn.**
Knit 3 rows.
Row 4 (WS): *P1, K1; rep from * to last 0 (1: 0: 0: 1: 0) st, P0 (1: 0: 0: 1: 0).
Row 5: P0 (1: 0: 0: 1: 0), *K1, P1; rep from * to end.
Rows 4 and 5 form moss st.
Work in moss st for 5 (5: 7: 7: 9: 9) rows more, ending with a WS row.
Dec 1 st at beg of next row and 2 foll 6th rows. 51 (54: 57: 61: 64: 69) sts.
Work 5 (5: 3: 3: 1: 1) rows, ending with a WS row.
Shaping side seam at same time, now work in textured stripe patt as folls:
Row 1 (RS): (K2, K2tog) 1 (1: 0: 0: 0: 0) times, K to last 8 sts, moss st 8 sts.

Row 2: Moss st 8 sts, P to end.
Row 3: (K2, K2tog) 0 (0: 1: 1: 0: 0) times, K to last 8 sts, moss st 8 sts.
Row 4: As row 2.
Row 5: (K2, K2tog) 0 (0: 0: 0: 1: 1) times, K to last 8 sts, moss st 8 sts.
Row 6: As row 2.
Rows 7 to 11: As rows 1 to 5.
49 (52: 55: 59: 62: 67) sts.
Row 12 (WS): *P1, K1; rep from * to last 1 (0: 1: 1: 0: 1) st, P1 (0: 1: 1: 0: 1).
Row 13: (Work 2 tog) 1 (1: 0: 0: 0: 0) times, K0 (1: 0: 0: 1: 0), *P1, K1; rep from * to last st, P1. 48 (51: 55: 59: 62: 67) sts.
Row 14: *P1, K1; rep from * to last 0 (1: 1: 1: 0: 1) st, P0 (1: 1: 1: 0: 1).
These 14 rows form patt and beg side seam shaping.

Place pocket

Next row (RS): (K2, K2tog) 0 (0: 1: 1: 0: 0) times, K9 (10: 8: 9: 13: 15), cast off next 21 (21: 23: 23: 25: 25) sts **firmly,** patt to end.
Next row: Patt 18 (20: 20: 23: 24: 27) sts, with WS facing purl across 21 (21: 23: 23: 25: 25) sts of first pocket lining, P to end. 48 (51: 54: 58: 62: 67) sts.
Working all side seam decreases as set, cont in patt, dec 1 st at each end of 3rd (3rd: 5th: 5th: next: next) and 0 (0: 0: 0: 1: 1) foll 6th row. 47 (50: 53: 57: 60: 65) sts.
Work 19 rows, ending with a WS row.
Next row (RS): Patt 2 sts, M1, patt to end. 48 (51: 54: 58: 61: 66) sts.
Working all side seam increases as set by last row, inc 1 st at beg of 6th (6th: 8th: 8th: 6th: 6th) and 1 (1: 0: 0: 0: 0) foll 6th row, then on 5 (5: 6: 6: 6: 6) foll 8th rows, taking inc sts into patt.
55 (58: 61: 65: 68: 73) sts.
Work 11 (11: 9: 9: 9: 9) rows, ending after patt row 4 (4: 8: 8: 8: 8) and with a WS row.

Shape armhole

Keeping patt correct, cast off 4 (4: 4: 4: 5: 5) sts at beg of next row.
51 (54: 57: 61: 63: 68) sts.
Work 1 row.
Dec 1 st at armhole edge of next 4 (5: 5: 6: 6: 8) rows, then on foll 3 (2: 3: 3: 3: 3) alt rows, and then on 0 (1: 1: 1: 1: 1) foll 4th row. 44 (46: 48: 51: 53: 56) sts.
Work 26 (25: 23: 24: 26: 28) rows, ending after patt row 14 (2: 6: 8: 10: 14) and with a WS row.

Shape neck

Next row (RS): Patt 27 (29: 30: 32: 34: 36) sts and turn, leaving rem 17 (17: 18: 19: 19: 20) sts on a holder.
Dec 1 st at neck edge of next 6 rows, then on foll 3 (4: 4: 4: 5: 5) alt rows, then on foll 4th row. 17 (18: 19: 21: 22: 24) sts.
Work 3 rows, ending after patt row 6 (10: 14: 2: 6: 10) and with a WS row.

Shape shoulder

Cast off 6 (6: 6: 7: 7: 8) sts at beg of next and foll alt row.
Work 1 row.
Cast off rem 5 (6: 7: 7: 8: 8) sts.
Mark positions for 6 buttons along left front opening edge – first to come in patt row 1, last to come in first row of neck shaping, and rem 4 buttons evenly spaced between.

RIGHT FRONT

Cast on 54 (57: 60: 64: 67: 72) sts using 3 ¼ mm (US 3) needles and main yarn.
Knit 3 rows.
Row 4 (WS): P0 (1: 0: 0: 1: 0), *K1, P1; rep from * to end.
Row 5: *P1, K1; rep from * to last 0 (1: 0: 0: 1: 0) st, P0 (1: 0: 0: 1: 0).
Rows 4 and 5 form moss st.
Work in moss st for 5 (5: 7: 7: 9: 9) rows more, ending with a WS row.
Dec 1 st at end of next row and 2 foll 6th rows. 51 (54: 57: 61: 64: 69) sts.
Work 5 (5: 3: 3: 1: 1) rows, ending with a WS row.
Shaping side seams at same time, now work in textured stripe patt as folls:
Row 1 (buttonhole row) (RS): P1, K1, P2tog tbl, (yrn) twice, K2tog (to make first buttonhole · on next row work twice into double yrn of previous row), moss st 2 sts, K to last 4 (4: 0: 0: 0: 0) sts, (K2tog tbl, K2) 1 (1: 0: 0: 0: 0) times.
Making a further 5 buttonholes in this way to correspond with positions marked for buttons on left front and noting that no further reference will be made to buttonholes, cont as folls:
Row 2: P to last 8 sts, moss st 8 sts.
Row 3: Moss st 8 sts, K to last 0 (0: 4: 4: 0: 0) sts, (K2tog tbl, K2) 0 (0: 1: 1: 0: 0) times.
Row 4: As row 2.
Row 5: Moss st 8 sts, K to last 0 (0: 0: 0: 4: 4) sts, (K2tog tbl, K2) 0 (0: 0: 0: 1: 1) times.

Row 6: As row 2.

Rows 7 to 11: As rows 1 to 5 but omitting buttonhole in row 1.
49 (52: 55: 59: 62: 67) sts.

Row 12 (WS): P1 (0: 1: 1: 0: 1), *K1, P1; rep from * to end.

Row 13: P1, *K1, P1; rep from * to last 2 (3: 0: 0: 1: 0) sts, K0 (1: 0: 0: 1: 0), (work 2 tog) 1 (1: 0: 0: 0: 0) times.
48 (51: 55: 59: 62: 67) sts.

Row 14: P0 (1: 1: 1: 0: 1), *K1, P1; rep from * to end.

These 14 rows form patt and beg side seam shaping.

Place pocket

Next row (RS): Patt 18 (20: 20: 23: 24: 27) sts, cast off next 21 (21: 23: 23: 25: 25) sts firmly, K to last 0 (0: 4: 4: 0: 0) sts, (K2tog tbl, K2) 0 (0: 1: 1: 0: 0) times.

Next row: K9 (10: 11: 12: 13: 15), with WS facing purl across 21 (21: 23: 23: 25: 25) sts of second pocket lining, patt to end. 48 (51: 54: 58: 62: 67) sts.

Complete to match left front, reversing shapings.

SLEEVES (both alike)

Cast on 67 (69: 71: 75: 79: 81) sts using 3 ¼ mm (US 3) needles and **contrast yarn**. Break off contrast yarn and join in **main yarn**.

Knit 3 rows.

Work in moss st as given for back for 11 rows, inc 1 st at each end of 6th row and ending with a WS row.
69 (71: 73: 77: 81: 83) sts.

Beg with patt row 1, now work in textured stripe patt (of 11 rows in st st followed by 3 rows in moss st) as given for back as folls:

Inc 1 st at each end of next (next: 3rd: 3rd: 3rd: 3rd) row. 71 (73: 75: 79: 83: 85) sts.

Work 3 (3: 5: 5: 5: 5) rows, ending after patt row 4 (4: 8: 8: 8: 8) and with a WS row.

Shape top

Keeping patt correct, cast off 4 (4: 4: 4: 5: 5) sts at beg next 2 rows.
63 (65: 67: 71: 73: 75) sts.

Dec 1 st at each end of next 3 rows, then on foll alt row, then on 5 (5: 5: 6: 6: 7) foll 4th rows. 45 (47: 49: 51: 53: 53) sts.

Work 1 row.

Dec 1 st at each end of next and foll 2 (5: 4: 3: 6: 4) alt rows, then on foll 7 (5: 7: 9: 7: 9) rows, end with a WS row. Cast off rem 25 sts.

MAKING UP

Join both shoulder seams using back stitch or mattress stitch if preferred.

Neck edging

With RS of right front facing, using 3 mm (US 2/3) needles and main colour, slip 17 (17: 18: 19: 19: 20) sts from right front holder onto right needle, rejoin yarn and pick up and knit 19 (21: 21: 21: 23: 23) sts up right side of neck, 43 (45: 47: 49: 51: 53) sts from back, and 19 (21: 21: 21: 23: 23) sts down left side of neck, then patt across 17 (17: 18: 19: 19: 20) sts on left front holder. 115 (121: 125: 129: 135: 139) sts.

Keeping moss st correct as set by front opening edge sts, work 6 rows in moss st across all sts, ending with a RS row.

Cast off in moss st (on **WS**). Join sleeve and side seams. Set sleeves into armholes.

Sew pocket linings in place on inside.

Sew on buttons.

53 (54: 55: 56: 57: 58) cm
20¾ (21¼: 21½: 22: 22½: 22¾) in

38 (40.5: 43: 45.5: 48: 52) cm
15 (16: 17: 18: 19: 20½) in

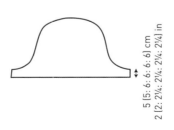

5 (5: 6: 6: 6: 6) cm
2 (2: 2¼: 2¼: 2¼: 2¼) in

DEVON
SLOUCHY STRIPED SWEATER

Recommendation

Suitable for the knitter with a little experience.
Please see page 46 for photograph.

	XS	S	M	L	XL	XXL	
To fit	**81**	**86**	**91**	**97**	**102**	**109**	**cm**
bust	32	34	36	38	40	43	in

Rowan Classic Pima Cotton DK

A	5	5	6	6	7	7	x 50g
B	3	3	4	4	4	5	x 50g

Photographed in Peppercorn & Badger

Needles

3mm (no 11) (US 2/3) circular needle
1 pair 3 ¾mm (no 9) (US 5) needles

Tension

23 sts and 30 rows to 10 cm measured over
stocking stitch using 3 ¾mm (US 5) needles.

BACK

Cast on 105 (111: 117: 121: 127: 137) sts
using 3 ¾mm (US 5) needles and shade A
(dark grey) and work as folls:
Row 1 (RS): K1 (1: 1: 0: 0: 2), (P1, K2)
to last 2 (2: 2: 1: 1: 3) sts, P1, K1 (1: 1:
0: 0: 2).
Row 2: P1 (1: 1: 0: 0: 2), (K1, P2) to last 2 (2:
2: 1: 1: 3) sts, K1, P1 (1: 1: 0: 0: 2).
These 2 rows form rib.
Work in rib for 14 (14: 16: 16: 18: 18) more
rows, ending with a WS row.
This completes the rib.
Beg with a K row, work in st st for 2 rows,
ending with a WS row.
Join in shade B (light grey) and cont in striped
st st as folls:
Work 6 rows using shade B (light grey).
Work 6 rows using shade A (dark grey).
The last 12 rows form striped st st and are
rep throughout.
Cont straight until work measures 22 cm,
ending with a WS row.

Shape underarm

Keeping stripes correct, inc 1 st at each end
of next and foll 10th row, then on foll 8th row,
then on foll 6th row, then on foll 4th row, then
on foll 4 alt rows.
123 (129: 135: 139: 145: 155) sts.
Work 1 row, ending with a WS row.
Cast on 3 sts at beg of next 2 rows, then
4 sts at beg of foll 4 rows.
145 (151: 157: 161: 167: 177) sts.

Place markers at both ends of last row to
denote base of armhole opening.
Cont straight until work measures 15 (16:
17: 17: 18: 19) cm from markers, ending
with a WS row.

Shape neck

Next row (RS): K55 (57: 59: 61: 63: 67)
and turn, leaving rem sts on a holder.
Work each side of neck separately.
Keeping stripes correct, dec 1 st at neck edge
of next 6 rows, then on foll 4 (4: 4: 5: 5: 5) alt
rows, then on 2 foll 6th rows.
43 (45: 47: 48: 50: 54) sts.
Cont straight until armhole measures
24 (25: 26: 27: 28: 29) cm from markers,
ending with a WS row.**
Leave these sts on a spare needle – the
shoulders will be grafted together.
With RS facing, rejoin appropriate yarn to rem
sts, cast off centre 35 (37: 39: 39: 41: 43)
sts, K to end. Complete to match first side,
reversing shapings.

FRONT

Work as for back to **.

Join left shoulder seam

Holding WS of back against WS of front,
join left shoulder seam by casting off
shoulder sts of both sections together,
by taking one st from front together with
one st from back throughout.
Complete front to match back, joining right
shoulder seam in the same way.

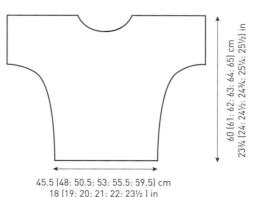

45.5 (48: 50.5: 53: 55.5: 59.5) cm
18 (19: 20: 21: 22: 23½) in

60 (61: 62: 63: 64: 65) cm
23¾ (24: 24½: 24¾: 25¼: 25½) in

MAKING UP

Pin out pieces and press carefully following instructions on ball band.

Neck edging

With RS facing, using 3mm (US 2/3) circular needle and shade A (dark grey), starting and ending at left shoulder seam, pick up and knit 26 (26: 26: 28: 28: 28) sts down left side of front neck, 35 (37: 38: 39: 40: 43) sts from front, 26 (26: 26: 28: 28: 28) sts up right side of front neck, 26 (26: 26: 28: 28: 28) sts down right side of back neck, 35 (36: 38: 38: 40: 43) sts from back, then 26 (26: 26: 28: 28: 28) sts up left side of back neck.

174 (177: 180: 189: 192: 198) sts.

Round 1 (RS): *K2, P1; rep from * to end.

Rep this round 8 times more.

Cast off in rib.

Armhole edgings (both alike)

With RS facing, using 3 ¾mm (US 5) needles and shade A (dark grey), pick up and knit 119 (125: 128: 134: 137: 143) sts evenly along straight row-end edge of armhole opening between markers.

Row 1 (WS): P2, *K1, P2; rep from * to end.

Row 2: K2, *P1, K2; rep from * to end.

These 2 rows form rib.

Work in rib for 13 (13: 15: 15: 17: 17) rows more, ending with a WS row.

Cast off in rib.

Join side and armhole border seams.

BAY
CARDIGAN WITH FLOUNCE & GARTER STITCH TRIM

Recommendation
Suitable for the knitter with a little experience.
Please see pages 44 & 47 for photographs.

	XS	S	M	L	XL	XXL	
To fit	**81**	**86**	**91**	**97**	**102**	**107**	cm
bust	32	34	36	38	40	42	in

Rowan Denim
12 13 14 15 16 17 x 50gm
Photographed in Nashville

Buttons – 7

Needles
1 pair 3 ¼ mm (no 10) (US 3) needles
1 pair 4 mm (no 8) (US 6) needles

Tension
Before washing: 20 sts and 28 rows to 10 cm
measured over stocking stitch using 4 mm
(US 6) needles.

Tension note: Denim will shrink in length
when washed for the first time. Allowances
have been made in the pattern for shrinkage
(see size diagram for after washing
measurements).

BACK
Cast on 139 (147: 159: 167: 179: 195) sts
using 4 mm (US 6) needles and work lower
frill as folls:
Work 6 (6: 6: 8: 8: 8) rows in garter st, i.e.
knit every row, ending with a WS row.
Beg with a K row, cont in st st until back
measures 14 (14: 14: 15: 15: 15) cm from
cast on edge, ending with a WS row.
Change to 3 ¼ mm (US 3) needles.
Next row (RS)(dec): K4, * (K3tog, K1) to last
3 sts, K3. 73 (77: 83: 87: 93: 101) sts.
Work 5 rows, ending with a WS row.
Change to 4mm (US 6) needles.
Work 4 rows.
Next row (RS)(inc): K2, M1, K to last 2 sts,
M1, K2. 75 (79: 85: 89: 95: 103) sts.
Work 7 rows.
Inc 1 st as before at each end of next row
and every foll 8th row to 87 (91: 97: 101:
107: 115) sts.
Work straight until back measures 25.5 (25.5:
27: 27: 27: 27) cm from **top of frill**, ending
with a WS row.
Shape armholes
Cast off 4 sts at beg of next 2 rows.
79 (83: 89: 93: 99: 107) sts.
Dec 1 st at each end of next 5 (5: 5: 5: 7: 7)
rows, then on 2 (3: 4: 5: 3: 6) foll alt rows,
and then on 1 (1: 1: 1: 2: 2) foll 4th rows.
63 (65: 69: 71: 75: 77) sts.
Work straight until armhole measures
21 (22: 22: 23.5: 24.5: 25.5) cm,
ending with a WS row.
Shape shoulders and back neck
Cast off 5 sts at beg of next 2 rows.
Cast off 4 (4: 5: 5: 5: 5) sts, K until 8 (8: 8: 8:
9: 9) sts on right needle and turn, leaving
rem sts on a holder.
Work each side of neck separately.
Cast off 4 sts, work to end.
Cast off rem 4 (4: 4: 4: 5: 5) sts.
With RS facing rejoin yarn to rem sts, cast off
centre 29 (31: 33: 35: 37: 39) sts, knit to end.
Complete to match first side, reversing
shapings.

LEFT FRONT
Cast on 72 (76: 81: 85: 91: 100) sts using
4 mm (US 6) needles and work lower frill,
setting sts as folls:
Work 6 (6: 6: 8: 8: 8) rows in garter st.
Next row (RS): Knit.
Next row: K9, P to end.
These 2 rows set the sts, i.e. 9 sts at centre
front worked in garter st for front band, and
rem sts worked in st st.
Keeping sts correct cont until work measures
14 (14: 14: 15: 15: 15) cm from cast on edge,
ending with a WS row.
Change to 3 ¼ mm (US 3) needles.
Next row (RS)(dec): K4, * (K3tog, K1) to last
12 (12: 13: 13: 13: 12) sts, K to end.
44 (46: 49: 51: 55: 58) sts.
Work 5 rows, dec 1 st at end of row on **XL
size only,** and ending with a WS row.
44 (46: 49: 51: 54: 58) sts.
Change to 4 mm (US 6) needles.
Work 4 rows.
Next row (RS)(inc): K2, M1, K to end.
45 (47: 50: 52: 55: 59) sts.
Work 7 rows, ending with a WS row.
Inc 1 st as before at beg of next row and every
foll 8th row to 51 (53: 56: 58: 61: 65) sts.
Work straight until left front matches back to
beg of armhole shaping, ending with
a WS row.
Shape armhole
Cast off 4 sts at beg of next row.
47 (49: 52: 54: 57: 61) sts.
Work 1 row.
Dec 1 st at armhole edge on next 5 (5: 5:
5: 7: 7) rows, then on 2 (3: 4: 5: 3: 6) foll
alt rows, and then on 1 (1: 1: 1: 2: 2) foll
4th rows.
39 (40: 42: 43: 45: 46) sts.
Work straight until front is 16 (16: 18: 18:
20: 20) rows shorter than back to beg of
shoulder shaping, ending with a WS row.
Shape front neck
Next row (RS): Knit 21 (21: 23: 23: 25: 25)
sts and turn, leaving rem 18 (19: 19: 20: 20:
21) sts on a holder for neckband.

Dec 1 st at neck edge on next 4 rows, then on 3 (3: 4: 4: 5: 5) foll alt rows, and then on foll 4th row. 13 (13: 14: 14: 15: 15) sts.
Work 1 row, ending with a WS row.

Shape shoulder
Cast off 5 sts at beg of next row and 4 (4: 5: 5: 5: 5) sts at beg of foll alt row.
Work 1 row.
Cast off rem 4 (4: 4: 4: 5: 5) sts.
Mark position of 5 buttons, first on the 3rd row after frill, the 5th 2 rows down from neck edge and rem 3 spaced evenly between.

RIGHT FRONT
Cast on 72 (76: 81: 85: 91: 100) sts using 4 mm (US 6) needles and work lower frill, setting sts as folls:
Work 6 (6: 6: 8: 8: 8) rows in garter st.
Next row (RS): Knit.
Next row: P to last 9 sts, K9.
These 2 rows set the sts, i.e. 9 sts at centre front worked in garter st for front band, and rem sts worked in st st.
Keeping sts correct cont until work measures 14 (14: 14: 15: 15: 15) cm from cast on edge, ending with a WS row.
Change to 3 ¼ mm (US 3) needles.
Next row (RS) (dec): K13 (13: 14: 14: 16: 13), (K3tog, K1) to last 3 sts, K3.
44 (46: 49: 51: 55: 58) sts.
Work 1 row, dec 1 st at beg of row on **XL size only.** 44 (46: 49: 51: 54: 58) sts.
Next row (RS)(buttonhole row): K3, K2tog tbl, (yon) twice, K2tog, K to end.

Next row: Work across row, knitting into the back of each loop made on previous row.
Work 2 rows, ending with a WS row.
Change to 4 mm (US 6) needles.
Work 4 rows.
Next row (RS)(inc): K to last 2 sts, M1, K2.
45 (47: 50: 52: 55: 59) sts.
Work 7 rows, ending with a WS row.
Complete to match left front, rev shapings and working buttonholes as before to correspond with positions marked for buttons.

LEFT SLEEVE
Sleeve front
Cast on 29 (30: 31: 33: 34: 35) sts using 3 ¼ mm (US 3) needles.
Work 8 (8: 8: 10: 10: 10) rows in garter st, ending with a WS row.
Next row (RS)(buttonhole row): K2, K2tog tbl, (yon) twice, K2tog, K to end.
Next row: Work across row, knitting into the back of each loop made on previous row.
Work a further 6 (6: 6: 8: 8: 8) rows in garter st, ending with a WS row.
Break yarn and leave sts on a spare needle.

SLEEVE BACK
Cast on 19 (20: 21: 23: 24: 25) sts using 3 ¼ mm (US 3) needles.
Work 16 (16: 16: 20: 20: 20) rows in garter st, ending with a WS row.
Do not break yarn.
Join sleeve front & back
Working on sts for sleeve back, knit to last

7 sts, now holding sleeve back behind front and taking 1 st from each needle together, knit 7 sts, K to end. 41 (43: 45: 49: 51: 53) sts.
Change to 4 mm (US 6) needles and purl 1 row, ending with a WS row.
Beg with a K row, cont in st st as folls:
Next row (RS)(inc): K2, M1, K to last 2 sts, M1, K2. 43 (45: 47: 51: 53: 55) sts.
Work 13 rows.
Inc 1 st as before at each end of next row and 3 (3: 3: 5: 5: 5) foll 14th row and then every foll 12th to 59 (63: 65: 69: 71: 73) sts.
Work straight until sleeve measures 46.5 (48: 49: 50: 51.5: 52.5) cm from top of garter stitch cuff, ending with a WS row.
Shape sleeve top
Cast off 4 sts at beg of next 2 rows.
51 (55: 57: 61: 63: 65) sts.
Dec 1 st at each end of next 3 rows, then on foll alt row, and then on every foll 4th row to 29 (31: 33: 37: 37: 39) sts, end with a RS row.
Work 1 row.
Dec 1 st at each end of next row and 1 (1: 1: 3: 2: 2) foll alt rows and then on every foll row to 19 (21: 23: 23: 25: 27) sts. Cast off.

RIGHT SLEEVE
Sleeve back
Cast on 19 (20: 21: 23: 24: 25) sts using 3 ¼ mm (US 3) needles.
Work 16 (16: 16: 20: 20: 20) rows in garter st, ending with a WS row.
Break yarn and leave sts on a spare needle.

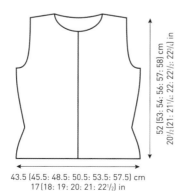

43.5 (45.5: 48.5: 50.5: 53.5: 57.5) cm
17 (18: 19: 20: 21: 22½) in

52 (53: 54: 56: 57: 58) cm
20½ (21: 21¼: 22: 22½: 22¾) in

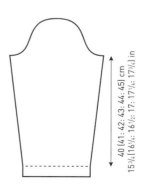

40 (41: 42: 43: 44: 45) cm
15¾ (16¼: 16½: 17: 17¼: 17¾) in

Continued on following page...

ASH
STRIPED SLOUCHY HAT WITH GARTER STITCH BAND

Recommendation
Suitable for the novice knitter.
Please see pages 18, 48 & 52 for photographs.

To fit: Average size

Rowan Milk Cotton Fine
A   1 x 50gm ball
B   1 x 50gm ball
Photographed in Water Bomb/Jelly & Tutti Frutti/liquorice

Needles
1 pair 2 ¼ mm (no 13) (US 1) needles
1 pair 2 ¾ mm (no 12) (US 2) needles

Tension
30 sts and 44 rows to 10 cm measured stocking stitch using 2 ¾ mm (US 2) needles.

Special abbreviations:
Inc = inc 1 st, by purling into front and then into back of next st.

HAT
Lower edging
Cast on 131 sts using 2 ¼ mm (US 1) needles and yarn B.
Break off yarn B and join in yarn A.
Work 25 rows in garter st, i.e. K every row, ending with a **RS** row.
Next row (WS) (inc): (P1, inc in next st) to last st, P1.
196 sts.
Change to 2 ¾ mm (US 2) needles and cont in st st in stripe patt as folls:
Join in yarn B, and taking the yarn not in use loosely up the side of the knitting cont in stripe patt as folls:
Using yarn B, work 4 rows in st st.
Using yarn A, work 4 rows in st st.
These last 8 rows form the stripe pattern.
Rep the 8 row stripe sequence 6 times more, ending with 4 rows of yarn A.
Work 2 more rows in yarn B.
Keeping stripe pattern correct cont as folls:

Shape crown
Next row (dec): (K1, K2tog) to last st, K1.
131 sts.
Work 5 rows.
Next row (RS)(dec): (K1, K2tog) to last 2 sts, K2. 88 sts.
Work 5 rows.
Next row (RS)(dec): (K1, K2tog) to last st, K1.
59 sts.
Work 3 rows.
Next row (RS)(dec): (K2tog) to last st, K1.
30 sts.
Work 3 rows.
Next row (RS)(dec): (K2tog) to end. 15 sts.
Break yarn and thread through rem 15 sts.
Pull up tight and fasten off securely.
Join seam.

Bay — Continued from previous page...

Sleeve front
Cast on 29 (30: 31: 33: 34: 35) sts using 3 ¼ mm (US 3) needles.
Work 8 (8: 8: 10: 10: 10) rows in garter st, ending with a WS row.
Next row (RS)(buttonhole row): K2, K2tog tbl, (yon) twice, K2tog, K to end.
Next row: Work across row, knitting into back of each loop made on previous row.
Work a further 6 (6: 6: 8: 8: 8) rows in garter st, ending with a WS row.
Do not break yarn.
Join sleeve back & front
Working on sts for sleeve front, knit to last

7 sts, now holding sleeve back behind front and taking 1 st from each needle together, knit 6 sts, K to end.
41 (43: 45: 49: 51: 53) sts.
Complete as given for left sleeve.

MAKING UP
Join shoulder seams, using back stitch or mattress st if preferred.
Neck edging
With RS of right front facing and using 3 ¼ mm (US 3) needles, slip 18 (19: 19: 20: 20: 21) sts on holder onto the right needle, pick up and knit 20 (20: 22: 22:

24: 24) sts up right front neck, 37 (39: 41: 43: 45: 47) across back and 20 (20: 22: 22: 24: 24) sts down left front, knit 18 (19: 19: 20: 20: 21) sts on holder.
113 (117: 123: 127: 133: 137) sts.
Knit 10 rows, ending with a **RS** row.
Cast off knitwise (on WS).
Join side and sleeve seams (but do not sew sleeve into armhole until after washing).
Machine wash all pieces together before completing sewing-up.
Set sleeves into armholes.
Sew on buttons to correspond with buttonholes.

LILAC
FITTED CARDIGAN WITH LACE PEPLUM

Recommendation
Suitable for the knitter with a little experience.
Please see page 49 for photograph.

	XS	S	M	L	XL	XXL	
To fit	**81**	**86**	**91**	**97**	**102**	**107**	cm
bust	32	34	36	38	40	42	in

Rowan Organic Cotton 4ply
      6   7   7   7   8   8 x 50gm
Photographed in Yellowwood

Buttons – 11

Needles
1 pair 2 ¼ mm (no 13) (US 1) needles
1 pair 2 ¾ mm (no 12) (US 2) needles
Cable needle

Tension
21 sts and 42 rows to 10 cm measured over
pattern using 2 ¾ mm (US 2) needles.

Special abbreviation
MSP = Make small picot as folls: Cast on 1 st,
cast off 1 st.
MLP = Make large picot as folls: Cast on
2 sts, cast off 2 sts.

LOWER EDGING (worked in one piece)
Cast on 21 sts using 2 ¾ mm (US 2) needles.
Knit 1 row.
Next row (WS): K5, K2tog, K2, yfwd, K1,
K2tog, yfwd, K2tog, K1, yfwd, K6.
Now work in patt as folls:
Row 1 (RS): Sl 1, K5, yfwd, slip next yfwd, K2,
(K1, K1 tbl) in next yfwd, K3, slip next 2 sts
onto cable needle and leave at front of work,
K3, then K2 from cable needle, yfwd, K2tog,
K1. 23 sts.
Row 2: MLP, K until there are 7 sts on right
needle, K2tog, yfwd, K2tog, K4, (K1, P1) into
next 2 yfwd loops as though they were one st,
K6. 22 sts.
Row 3: Sl 1, K4, K2tog, yfwd, K2tog, K10,
yfwd, K2tog, K1. 21 sts.
Row 4: K5, (yfwd, K1) twice, K2tog, yfwd,
K2tog, K3, yfwd, drop next yfwd of previous
row off needle, K6. 22 sts.
Row 5: Sl 1, K5, (K1, P1) into next yfwd, K7,
(K1, K1 tbl) into next yfwd, K1, (K1, K1 tbl)
into next yfwd, K2, yfwd, K2tog, K1. 25 sts.
Row 6: MLP, K until there are 5 sts on right
needle, yfwd, K2, yfwd, K2tog, K1, yfwd, (K1,
K2tog, yfwd, K2tog) twice, K5.
Row 7: Sl 1, K5, yfwd, drop next yfwd of
previous row off needle, K6, (yfwd, K2tog, K1)
4 times.
Row 8: K5, (yfwd, K2tog, K1) 3 times, yfwd,
K2tog, K2, (K1, P1) into next yfwd, K6. 26 sts.
Row 9: Sl 1, K4, K2tog, yfwd, K2tog, K5,
(yfwd, K2tog, K1) 4 times. 25 sts.
Row 10: MLP, K until there are 5 sts on right
needle, (yfwd, K2tog, K1) 3 times, yfwd,
K2tog, K2, yfwd, drop next yfwd of previous
row off needle, K6.
Row 11: Sl 1, K5, (K1, P1) into next yfwd, K6,
(yfwd, K2tog, K1) 4 times. 26 sts.
Row 12: K5, (yfwd, K2tog, K1) 4 times, K2tog,
yfwd, K2tog, K5. 25 sts.
Row 13: As row 7.
Row 14: MLP, K until there are 5 sts on right
needle, (yfwd, K2tog, K1) 3 times, yfwd,
K2tog, K2, (K1, P1) into next yfwd, K6. 26 sts.
Row 15: As row 9. 25 sts.

Row 16: K5, (yfwd, K2tog, K1) 3 times, yfwd,
K2tog, K2, yfwd, drop next yfwd of previous
row off needle, K6.
Row 17: Sl 1, K5, (K1, P1) into next yfwd, K6,
yfwd, (K2tog, K1) twice, (yfwd, K2tog, K1)
twice.
Row 18: MLP, K until there are 5 sts on right
needle, yfwd, K2tog, K1, K2tog, yfwd, K2tog,
K1, yfwd, K3, K2tog, yfwd, K2tog, K5. 24 sts.
Row 19: Sl 1, K5, yfwd, drop next yfwd of
previous row off needle, K7, yfwd, K2tog, K2,
(yfwd, K2tog, K1) twice.
Row 20: K5, yfwd, (K2tog) twice, yfwd, K2tog,
K1, yfwd, K5, (K1, P1) into next yfwd, K6. 25 sts.
Row 21: Sl 1, K4, K2tog, yfwd, K2tog, K7,
(K2tog, K1) twice, yfwd, K2tog, K1. 22 sts.
Row 22: K5, K2tog, K2, yfwd, K1, K2tog,
yfwd, K2tog, K1, yfwd, drop next yfwd of
previous row off needle, K6. 21 sts.
These 22 rows form patt.
Rep last 22 rows 15 (16: 17: 18: 19: 21)
times more, then row 1 again, ending with a
RS row. 16 (17: 18: 19: 20: 22) full patt reps
and 355 (377: 399: 421: 443: 487) rows
worked in total.
Cast off.
Place markers along straight row-end edge
after 94 (100: 106: 112: 118: 132) rows from
cast-on and cast-off edges, leaving 167 (177:
187: 197: 207: 223) rows between markers.
Section between markers will be section used
for back, whilst sections beyond markers will
be used for fronts.

BACK
With RS facing and using 2 ¾ mm (US 2)
needles, pick up and knit 84 (89: 94: 99:
104: 112) evenly along straight (upper) row-
end edge of lower edging between markers
(this is 1 st for every 2 rows).
Next row (WS): K6 (3: 4: 4: 8: 7), K2tog, *K8
(8: 10: 9: 15: 17), K2tog; rep from * to last 6
(4: 4: 5: 9: 8) sts, K to end.
76 (80: 86: 90: 98: 106) sts.
Next row (eyelet row): K1, yfrn, P2tog, *yrn,
P2tog; rep from * to last st, K1.

Next row: Knit.

Now work in patt as folls:

Row 1 (RS): K1, yfrn, P2tog, *yrn, P2tog; rep from * to last st, K1.

Row 2: As row 1.

These 2 rows form patt.

Work 14 rows in patt, ending with a WS row.

Next row (inc) (RS): K into front, back and front again of first st, patt to last st, K into front, back and front again of last st. 80 (84: 90: 94: 102: 110) sts.

Working all side seam increases as set by last row, inc 2 sts at each end of 22nd and foll 22nd row, taking inc sts into patt. 88 (92: 98: 102: 110: 118) sts.

Cont straight until back measures 20 (21: 22: 22: 23: 23) cm **from pick-up row,** ending with a WS row.

Shape armholes

Keeping patt correct, cast off 4 sts **loosely** at beg of next 2 rows. 80 (84: 90: 94: 102: 110) sts.

Next row (dec) (RS): K3tog, patt to last 3 sts, K3tog tbl. 76 (80: 86: 90: 98: 106) sts.

Working all decreases as set by last row, dec 2 sts at each end of 4th and 1 (1: 2: 2: 2: 3) foll 4th rows.

68 (72: 74: 78: 86: 90) sts.

Cont straight until armhole measures 17 (18: 18: 19: 19: 20) cm, ending with a WS row.

Shape shoulders and back neck

Taking care not to cast off too tightly and keeping patt correct, cast off 5 (6: 6: 6: 8: 8) sts at beg of next 2 rows. 58 (60: 62: 66: 70: 74) sts.

Next row (RS): Cast off 5 (6: 6: 6: 8: 8) sts, patt until there are 9 (9: 10: 11: 11: 12) sts on right needle and turn, leaving rem sts on a holder.

Work each side of neck separately.

Cast off 4 sts at beg of next row.

Cast off rem 5 (5: 6: 7: 7: 8) sts.

With RS facing rejoin yarn to rem sts, cast off centre 30 (30: 30: 32: 32: 34) sts, patt to end.

Complete to match first side, reversing shapings.

LEFT FRONT

With RS facing and using 2 ¾ mm (US 2) needles, pick up and knit 47 (50: 53: 56: 59: 66) evenly along straight (upper) row-end edge of lower edging to left of back (this is 1 st for every 2 rows).

Next row (WS): K4 (4: 6: 5: 6: 5), K2tog, *K10 (8: 11: 9: 13: 7), K2tog; rep from * to last 5 (4: 6: 5: 6: 5) sts, K to end. 43 (45: 49: 51: 55: 59) sts.

Next row (eyelet row): K1, yfrn, P2tog, *yrn, P2tog; rep from * to last 2 sts, K2.

Next row: MSP, K to end.

Now work in patt as folls:

Row 1 (RS): K1, yfrn, P2tog, *yrn, P2tog; rep from * to last 2 sts, K2.

Row 2: MSP, K1 (2 sts now on right needle), yfrn, P2tog, *yrn, P2tog; rep from * to last st, K1.

These 2 rows set the sts – front opening edge 2 sts in garter st with small picots worked on every other row and rem sts in patt as given for back.

Cont as set for 14 rows more, ending with a WS row.

Working all increases as given for back, inc 2 sts at beg of next and 2 foll 22nd rows, taking inc sts into patt.

49 (51: 55: 57: 61: 65) sts.

Cont straight until left front matches back to beg of armhole shaping, ending with a WS row.

Shape armhole

Keeping patt correct, cast off 4 sts **loosely** at beg of next row. 45 (47: 51: 53: 57: 61) sts.

Work 1 row.

Working all decreases as set by back, dec 2 sts at beg of next and 2 (2: 3: 3: 3: 4) foll 4th rows.

39 (41: 43: 45: 49: 51) sts.

Cont straight until 25 rows less have been worked than on back to start of shoulder shaping, ending with a **RS** row.

Shape neck

Keeping patt correct, cast off 10 (10: 11: 12: 12: 13) sts **loosely** at beg of next row. 29 (31: 32: 33: 37: 38) sts.

Working all decreases as set by back, dec 2 sts at neck edge of next and foll 3 alt rows, then on 3 foll 4th rows. 15 (17: 18: 19: 23: 24) sts.

Work 5 rows, ending with a WS row.

Shape shoulder

Taking care not to cast off too tightly and keeping patt correct, cast off 5 (6: 6: 6: 8: 8) sts at beg of next and foll alt row.

Work 1 row.

Cast off rem 5 (5: 6: 7: 7: 8) sts.

RIGHT FRONT

With RS facing and using 2 ¾ mm (US 2) needles, pick up and knit 47 (50: 53: 56: 59: 66) evenly along rem straight (upper) row-end edge of lower edging to right of back (this is 1 st for every 2 rows).

Next row (WS): K4 (4: 6: 5: 6: 5), K2tog, *K10 (8: 11: 9: 13: 7), K2tog; rep from * to last 5 (4: 6: 5: 6: 5) sts, K to end. 43 (45: 49: 51: 55: 59) sts.

Next row (eyelet row): MSP, K1 (2 sts now on right needle), yfrn, P2tog, *yrn, P2tog; rep from * to last st, K1.

Next row: Knit.

Now work in patt as folls:

Row 1 (RS): MSP, K1 (2 sts now on right needle), yfrn, P2tog, *yrn, P2tog; rep from * to last st, K1.

Row 2: K1, yfrn, P2tog, *yrn, P2tog; rep from * to last 2 sts, K2.

These 2 rows set the sts – front opening edge 2 sts in garter st with small picots worked on every other row and rem sts in patt as given for back.

Complete to match left front, reversing shapings.

SLEEVES (both alike)
First section

Using 2 ¾ mm (US 2) needles, work picot cast-on as folls: cast on 4 sts, cast off 1 st, slip st now on right needle back onto left needle, *cast on 3 sts, cast off 1 st, slip st now on right needle back onto left needle; rep from * until there are 27 (29: 29: 31: 31: 31) sts on left needle, cast on 1 st.

28 (30: 30: 32: 32: 32) sts.**

Row 1 (RS): MSP, K to end.

Row 2: Knit.

Rows 3 and 4: As rows 1 and 2.

Row 5: As row 1.

Row 6: K4, K2tog, (K7 (8: 8: 9: 9: 9), K2tog) twice, K4. 25 (27: 27: 29: 29: 29) sts.

Now work in patt as folls:

Row 1 (RS): MSP, K1 (2 sts now on right needle), yfrn, P2tog, *yrn, P2tog; rep from * to last st, K1.

Row 2: K1, yfrn, P2tog, *yrn, P2tog; rep from * to last 2 sts, K2.

These 2 rows set the sts – opening edge 2 sts in garter st with small picots worked on every other row and rem sts in patt as given for back.

Cont as set for 15 rows more, ending with a **RS** row.

Next row (WS): Patt to last 2 sts, P2tog. 24 (26: 26: 28: 28: 28) sts.
Break yarn and leave sts on a spare needle.

Second section
Work as given for first section to **.
Row 1 (RS): Knit.
Row 2: MSP, K to end.
Rows 3 and 4: As rows 1 and 2.
Row 5: As row 1.
Row 6: MSP, K until there are 4 sts on right needle, K2tog, (K7 (8: 8: 9: 9: 9), K2tog) twice, K4. 25 (27: 27: 29: 29: 29) sts.
Now work in patt as folls:
Row 1 (RS): K1, yfrn, P2tog, *yrn, P2tog; rep from * to last 2 sts, K2.
Row 2: MSP, K1 (2 sts now on right needle), yfrn, P2tog, *yrn, P2tog; rep from * to last st, K1.
These 2 rows set the sts – opening edge 2 sts in garter st with small picots worked on every other row and rem sts in patt as given for back.
Cont as set for 15 rows more, ending with a **RS** row.
Next row (WS): P2tog, patt to end. 24 (26: 26: 28: 28: 28) sts.
Do not break yarn.

Join sections
Next row (RS): Patt 24 (26: 26: 28: 28: 28) sts of second section, then keeping patt correct patt 24 (26: 26: 28: 28: 28) sts of first section. 48 (52: 52: 56: 56: 56) sts.
Keeping patt correct, work 9 (9: 5: 11: 7: 7) rows, ending with a WS row.
Working all increases as set by back, inc 2 sts at each end of next and 2 (3: 3: 3: 4: 4) foll 28th (30th: 24th: 32nd: 26th: 26th) rows, then on 1 (0: 1: 0: 0: 0) foll 30th (0: 26th: 0: 0: 0) row, taking inc sts into patt. 64 (68: 72: 72: 76: 76) sts.
Work straight until sleeve measures 32 (33: 34: 35: 36: 36) cm, ending with a WS row.

Shape sleeve top
Keeping patt correct, cast off 4 sts **loosely** at beg of next 2 rows.
56 (60: 64: 64: 68: 68) sts.
Working all decreases in same way as given for back armhole decreases, dec 2 sts at each end of next and foll 4th row, then on 3 foll 10th rows, then on 2 (2: 2: 2: 2: 3) foll 6th rows, then on 1 (2: 2: 2: 2: 2) foll 4th rows, then on foll alt row.
20 (20: 24: 24: 28: 24) sts.
Work 1 row, ending with a WS row.
Cast off.

MAKING UP
Press all pieces using a warm iron over a damp cloth.
Join both shoulder seams using back stitch or mattress st if preferred.

Neck edging
With RS facing and using 2 ¼ mm (US 1) needles, beg and ending at front opening edges, pick up and knit 28 (30: 30: 30: 30: 30) sts up right side of neck, 45 (45: 45: 47: 47: 51) sts from back, then 28 (30: 30: 30: 30: 30) sts down left side of neck. 101 (105: 105: 107: 107: 111) sts.
Row 1 (WS): MSP, K to end.
Rep this row twice more, ending with a WS row.
Now work picot cast-off as folls: Cast off 2 sts, (slip st on right needle back onto left needle, cast on 2 sts, cast off 4 sts) to end.
Join sleeve and side seams.
Set sleeves into armholes.
Using "holes" of edge vertical row of patt of right front as buttonholes, attach 9 buttons to left front opening edge – place first button level with eyelet row, last button just below neck shaping, and rem 7 buttons evenly spaced between.
Make button loop at front edge of garter st rows of sleeve section and attach button to back sleeve section to correspond.

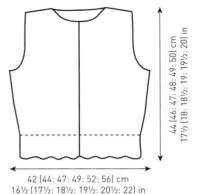

44 (46: 47: 48: 49: 50) cm
17½ (18: 18½: 19: 19½: 20) in

42 (44: 47: 49: 52: 56) cm
16½ (17½: 18½: 19½: 20½: 22) in

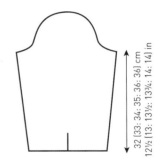

32 (33: 34: 35: 36: 36) cm
12½ (13: 13½: 13¾: 14: 14) in

INFORMATION
A GUIDE TO ASSIST WITH TECHNIQUES & FINISHING TOUCHES

TENSION

Achieving the correct tension has to be one of the most important elements in producing a beautiful, well fitting knitted garment. The tension controls the size and shape of your finished piece and any variation to either stitches or rows, however slight, will affect your work and change the fit completely. To avoid any disappointment, we would always recommend that you knit a tension square in the yarn and stitch given in the pattern, working perhaps four or five more stitches and rows than those given in the tension note.

When counting the tension, place your knitting on a flat surface and mark out a 10cm square with pins. Count the stitches between the pins. If you have too many stitches to 10cm your knitting it too tight, try again using thicker needles, if you have too few stitches to 10cm your knitting is too loose, so try again using finer needles. Please note, if you are unable to achieve the correct stitches and rows required, the stitches are more crucial as many patterns are knitted to length.
Keep an eye on your tension during knitting, especially if you're going back to work which has been put to one side for any length of time.

SIZING

The instructions are given for the smallest size. Where they vary, work the figures in brackets for the larger sizes. One set of figures refers to all sizes. The size diagram with each pattern will help you decide which size to knit. The measurements given on the size diagram are the actual size your garment should be when completed. Measurements will vary from design to design because the necessary ease allowances have been made in each pattern to give your garment the correct fit, i.e. a

loose fitting garment will be several cm wider than a neat fitted one, a snug fitting garment may have no ease at all.

WORKING A LACE PATTERN

When working a lace pattern it is important to remember that if you are unable to work a full repeat i.e. both the increase and corresponding decrease and vice versa, the stitches should be worked in stocking stitch or an alternative stitch suggested in the pattern.

CHART NOTE

Some of our patterns include a chart. Each square on a chart represent a stitch and each line of squares a row of knitting.

When working from a chart, unless otherwise stated, read odd rows (RS) from right to left and even rows (WS) from left to right. The key alongside each chart indicates how each stitch is worked.

FINISHING INSTRUCTIONS

It is the pressing and finishing which will transform your knitted pieces into a garment to be proud of.

Pressing

Darn in ends neatly along the selvage edge. Follow closely any special instructions given on the pattern or ball band and always take great care not to over press your work. Block out your knitting on a pressing or ironing board, easing into shape, and unless otherwise states, press each piece using a warm iron over a damp cloth.

Tip: Attention should be given to ribs/edgings; if the garment is close fitting – steam the ribs gently so that the stitches fill out but stay elastic. Alternatively if the garment is to hang straight then steam out to the correct shape.

Tip: Take special care to press the selvages, as this will make sewing up both easier and neater.

CONSTRUCTION
Stitching together

When stitching the pieces together, remember to match areas of pattern very carefully where they meet. Use a stitch such as back stitch or mattress stitch for all main knitting seams and join all ribs and neckband with mattress stitch, unless otherwise stated.
Take extra care when stitching the edgings and collars around the back neck of a garment. They control the width of the back neck, and if too wide the garment will be ill fitting and drop off the shoulder. Knit back neck edgings only to the length stated in the pattern, even stretching it slightly if for example, you are working in garter or horizontal rib stitch.
Stitch edgings/collars firmly into place using a back stitch seam, easing-in the back neck to fit the collar/edging rather than stretching the collar/edging to fit the back neck.

Set-in sleeves: Join side and sleeve seams. Place centre of cast off edge of sleeve to shoulder seams. Set in sleeve, easing sleeve head into armhole.

CARE INSTRUCTIONS
Yarns

Follow the care instructions printed on each individual ball band. Where different yarns are used in the same garment, follow the care instructions for the more delicate one.

Buttons

We recommend that buttons are removed if your garment is to be machine washed.

CROCHET

We are aware that crochet terminology varies from country to country. Please note we have used the English style in this publication.

Crochet abbreviations

ch	chain
ss	slip stitch
dc	double crochet
htr	half treble
tr	treble
dtr	double treble
htr2tog	half treble 2tog
tr2tog	treble 2tog
yoh	yarn over hook
sp(s)	space(s)

Double crochet

1 Insert the hook into the work (as indicated in the pattern), wrap the yarn over the hook and draw the yarn through the work only.
2 Wrap the yarn again and draw the yarn through both loops on the hook.
3 1 dc made

Half treble

1 Wrap the yarn over the hook & insert the hook into the work (as indicated in pattern).
2 Wrap the yarn over the hook draw through the work only and wrap the yarn again.
3 Draw through all 3 loops on the hook.
4 1 half treble made.

Treble

1 Wrap the yarn over the hook and insert the hook into the work (as indicated on the pattern).
2 Wrap the yarn over the hook draw through the work only and wrap the yarn again.
3 Draw through the first 2 loops only and wrap the yarn again.
4 Draw through the last 2 loops on the hook.
5 1 treble made.

ABBREVIATIONS

K	knit
P	purl
K1b	knit 1 through back loop
st(s)	stitch(es)
inc	increas(e)(ing)
dec	decreas(e)(ing)
st st	stocking stitch (1 row K, 1 row P)
garter st	garter stitch (K every row)
beg	begin(ning)
foll	following
rem	remain(ing)
rev st st	reverse stocking stitch (1 row P, 1 row K)
rep	repeat
alt	alternate
cont	continue
patt	pattern
tog	together
mm	millimetres
cm	centimetres
in(s)	inch(es)
RS	right side
WS	wrong side
sl 1	slip one stitch
psso	pass slipped stitch over
tbl	through back of loop
M1	make one stitch by picking up horizontal loop before next stitch and knitting into back of it
M1p	make one stitch by picking up horizontal loop before next stitch and purling into back of it
yfwd	yarn forward
yon	yarn over needle
yrn	yarn round needle
MP	Make picot: Cast on 1 st, by inserting the right needle between the first and second stitch on left needle, take yarn round needle, bring loop through and place on left (one stitch cast on), cast off 1 st, by knitting first the loop and then the next stitch, pass the first stitch over the second (one stitch cast off).
Cn	cable needle
C4B	Cable 4 back: Slip next 2 sts onto a cn and hold at back of work, K2, K2 from cn.
C4F	Cable 4 front: Slip next 2 sts onto a cn and hold at front of work, K2, K2 from cn.

THANK YOU!

Graham Watts, Diana Fisher, Hannah Wright, Kristie Stubley
Angela Lin, Sue Whiting, Trisha McKenzie, Susan Laybourn
Ella Taylor, Arna Ronan, Sandra Richardson,
Amanda Crawford, Ann Hinchcliffe, & Lindsay Hargreaves

Gill and all members of Thurstonland C.C.

INDEX